Philosophy is not Difficult ... We Are!

THINKING ABOUT WHO AND WHAT WE ARE

Robert Gilgulin

Copyright © 2024 by Robert Gilgulin

All rights reserved. No part of this book may be reproduced in any manner whatsoever without written permission except in the case of brief quotations embodied in critical articles and reviews.

First Printing, 2024

Cover image used under license from Shutterstock.com

ISBN 979-8-218-46265-9 (paperback)
ISBN 979-8-218-46266-6 (ebook)

R&T Publishing, Colorado

PHILOSOPHY IS NOT
DIFFICULT ... WE ARE!

Contents

Introduction	vii
On the Right	1
Classic, Romantic	8
Character	14
A Serious Person	19
I Feel Like ...	26
Persuasion	37
Ambiguous, Ambivalent	42
A Note on Denoting	49
Atom	54
Things	59
Is Existence Overrated?	67
Is Existence a Proper Predicate?	80
Is Seeing Believing?	87
Sense and Sensibility	93
Cause	101
Out There, Part One	114
Out There, Part Two	120

Out There, Part Three	128
I Have an Idea	139
Knowability	152
Sophistication	162
High Moments	167
Three Awful Dogmas	177
Philosophy is Not Difficult ... We Are!	187
Can Philosophy Change Your Life?	200
Certainty	206
Words	214
Does God Exist?	227
Played All the Cards in His Hand	233
The End	240
Acknowledgement	243

Introduction

1. Avoid the tedium of a textbook. Here's a nicer, neater, quicker glimpse into what philosophers think.

Oh, no! Don't try a cover to cover read. You would drown in repetition. I hope you are the pro-active reader who always first looks at the last page to determine, right away, if a book is for you.

Test it before you commit your time and attention. Pick a title that tickles. Thirty essays; thirty portals; peek in here and there before you decide to visit. So varied are philosophical views! Which is for you? Which satisfies and deserves your attention?

2. Are you the analytical sort, bothered by lack of precision, and desiring demonstrated significant results? Or are you more attracted to the flavor of things? Your character is explored in the second essay, **Classic, Romantic**.

Ah! **Character**, third essay: *The Greeks know that life is hard. For most peoples, nothing to do about it. For the Greeks...*

Probably controversial is **A Serious Person**: *In The Godfather, Marlon Brando portrays a dark but serious person ... all within a moral code to which he is more faithful than the average American is to our Constitution. His sense of right and wrong dominates all he does. Superman gives the bad guys a* *quick and final kibosh and is unfettered by due process. That doesn't bother us at all.* How committed are you to your sense of right and wrong?

The first essay begins: *When did our schools begin to rot? When they stopped teaching shop class. In shop class we learned there is a right way to do things. In philosophy class we learn ...*

These four are for *getting acquainted*. Taste before you bite off a mouthful, and a mindful. Remember Orwell: *A good book tells you what you already know*. First test its timbre. Proceed if its tone resonates congenially.

3. If you decide to make a path through these essays, notice these signposts:

When done well, philosophy does not find answers to its questions, but when the question is better understood, more intriguing questions are uncovered. Let's not expect answers, but a better understanding of the question.

So unlike one another in goal and method, the various philosophical views can hardly speak to or understand one another. We take a path into both the English-speaking analytic way and the continental, French and German, existentialist, phenomenological way. *Me? I lean to the latter.*

These essays are tilted and stilted by my own view that: *How you say it determines what you say.* This against the ordinary view that what you say is determined by whatever it is that you are speaking about.

On the Right

Men are born ignorant, not stupid. They are made stupid by education.

Bertrand Russell, *A History of Western Philosophy.*

1. When did our schools begin to rot? When we stopped teaching *shop* class.

The point was not for Junior to bring home an ash tray or a spice rack, but to bring a sense that there is a right way to do things. Only if first experienced, then practiced and mastered, does one learn *there is a right way to do things* and only then can one transcend mechanical proficiency to an appreciation of this new understanding of our world, the world revealed by its inherent and intrinsic value, moral and aesthetic.

From the *right*, as in *the right way to do things*, to the *Right-itself*, that's how we come to know that objective value, both moral and aesthetic, determines the world.

How to meet the *Right-itself*, the *Good* and the *Beautiful* and the *Excellent*, as a stand-alone substantial entity? Tie your shoelaces with such verve and elegance that then you can move toward *Elegance-itself*. If our early experiences do not teach that there is a right way to do things, then, chances are, we will fall to the default position: Value, both moral and aesthetic, is but whim, subjective opinion and personal preference.

In home economics, students learned to cook, sew, make a bed, and were brought to the necessary first life experience that there is *a right way to do it*. And *the right way to do things* must be experienced, must be lived, or we dare not ask: *Is there a right way to live?*

2. I am not the first to say this. Two and a half thousand years ago, Socrates proclaimed against the prominent Sophists, the self-centered cultural persuasion of his time, that the unexamined life is not worth living. The important word here is *worth*. The ultimate purpose of being a person, and not just another species of sentient creature, is the discovery that we are to appreciate *Worthiness itself*.

In *Closing of the American Mind,* Allan Bloom says that students coming into his University of Chicago classes are certain that truth is relative. They think truth is a subjective thing, a matter of opinion, something personal, of no objective force, a function of the mental event that thinks it. Postmodern and very tolerant of each other, they allow themselves the contradictory notion of *my truth* as in *true to (him, her) them*.

The mark and measure of these postmodern times, tolerant of any view, even evil ones: *Truth* is relative, and as relative are the notions of *the Good, the Excellent* and *the Beautiful,* all tossed into the dustbin of casual self-serving personal preference.

Bloom laments that none of his students know to prospect for the *Elegant itself,* the *Excellent itself,* the exquisite. They do not know that the *Beautiful* and the *Sublime* are the most important objectives, and reside in the realm of universal truth, available only to those who seek them out, and more valuable than gold.

3. Childish and egotistical relativism mark every beginning both for individuals and for civilizations. Early on, the child cannot see past their own impressions, feelings and needs. True of each child and every civilization, at their beginning they must work on what *works*. Early

childhood and early civilization must organize the doing of things. After that, perhaps, grow to an appreciation of universal, objective truth.

At their beginning, each child, and every civilization, must suffer the tension between what works and what is worthy. First, *what works,* then, the lived experience that *there is a right way to do things* invites reflection on the *Right* itself, then on the *Good* and the *Beautiful* themselves.

4. First, meet the demands of common sense: *learn how to do things.* And you cannot miss this on-the-job lesson: there is a right and a wrong way. The next step forward, as the Greeks would say, from *practikai* to *theoria,* from the practical to the theoretical, from doing your task to judging your work; from meeting the demand of day-in and day-out living to estimating if what you have done has, or has not, been done well.

Was it worth doing?

This distinguishes us from all other creatures. The human soul needs to quench its thirst with a taste of the Excellent, for Good over Evil, for *Worthiness-itself.*

5. Accomplishing and achieving something practical awakens consideration of *Accomplishment-itself.* An important insight into the nature of reality: *How well-done is a thing? How good a one is it?* Is that not how real it is? The *better* one ... is that not the more *real* one? And the better one is more beautiful ... correct?

What comes next is *Beauty-itself,* not just a piece of preference, not just a sentiment, not a matter of opinion, but the foundation and explanation, the Rosetta Stone that unlocks and makes available objective reality itself.

6. All creatures do things. Only you and I can ask: *can it be done better?* In shop class we learned that there is a right way to do things. In philosophy class we learn this: *How-well-accomplished-and-achieved* and *how-good-a-one-of-its-kind* measures how real is a thing.

The realization that there are good ones and, too, better ones, leads us to think about *the best possible one*. It's a shame that in mundane and ordinary day-in and day-out living we will never encounter *the best possible one*. But by moving beyond *doing* to *judging* we will discover our proper goal: *Aim for the best!* That is how and why the Greeks invented Olympic sport.

Search out the best runner, best wrestler, best discus-thrower. And, of course, the best deserves to be immortalized in the world's most accomplished sculpture. (Time now to look at the ancient *Artemision Bronze and Laocoön and His Sons*.) Yes. The search for the best among us ordinary fellows leads to the discovery of the Beautiful and the Sublime as the metric for reality itself.

We come to realize that *That's a beautiful one!* is not the simple, childish expression of personal preference, but an attempt at objective, universal, metaphysical truth.

7. The first great philosophical debate, fifth century B.C. Athens, between the Sophists, champions of common sense and practical success, and Socrates, champion of *Worthiness*. The Dale Carnegies of their day, the Sophists trained their students in the art of *winning*, by any means necessary, especially by rhetorical trickery. Socrates directed everyone's attention to worthiness as the proper goal of life, even if the search for worthiness and the good and the beautiful could be an obstacle to personal success.

Nothing is either good or bad, argues the Sophist Protagoras, *but thinking so makes it so*. Bloom's incoming freshmen would agree. The point is not to allow concern for truth and objectivity to stand in the way of winning. Winning what? Success, status, influence and popularity: each, of course, in the service of the others.

The nineteenth century philosopher, Friedrick Nietzsche, raises the ego-centric sophist impulse to romantic excess with his:

> *There are no facts, only interpretations; I would believe only in a God that knows how to Dance; We have art in order not to die of the truth; There are no moral phenomena at all, but only a moral interpretation of phenomena.*

8. Out of this titanic struggle (Sophism vs. Socrates) Western Civilization is born. The most famous Sophists, from Protagoras and Gorgias through Thrasymachus taught *shop*, taught men how to succeed in all manner of practical affairs. Relativism (*truth is relative to each man's choice of his favorite beliefs*), becomes the benchmark of the practical man and the Sophist mantra: *Man is measure of all things.*

Socrates' student, Plato, taught that all that *is*, is objective and made real by the measure of the *Good* itself, and the *Beautiful,* not just a personal predilection, but the measure of how real a thing is. *How real?* Isn't that the same as *How Good?* Socrates and Plato helped the Greeks develop their natural instincts and native talent for seeking the excellent in all things.

> *The Greeks, according to Nietzsche in* **Birth of Tragedy,** *knew very well that life is terrible, inexplicable, dangerous. But though they were alive to the real character of the nature of the world and of human life, they did not surrender to pessimism by turning their backs on life ... There were, however, two ways of doing this, corresponding respectively to the Dionysian and Apollonian Attitudes or mentalities. ... The ideal*

> *world of form and beauty, this is the Apollonian way. ... The other possibility is that of triumphantly affirming and embracing existence in all its darkness and horror. This is the Dionysian attitude, and its typical art forms are tragedy and music. And they then were able to say yes to the world as an aesthetic medium of art.*
>
> Fr. Copleston, "Nietzsche," *The History of Philosophy*, Vol. 7.

Sophistry has come to signify the deliberate use of fallacious reasoning, intellectual charlatanism and moral unscrupulousness. (Internet Encyclopedia of Philosophy)

Socrates taught men to know that the only life worth living is an examined life which prizes excellence.

9. Aristotle, student of the Socratic Plato, asks:

> *Have the carpenter, then, and the tanner certain functions or activities, and has man none? Is he born without a function?*
>
> *Nichomachean Ethics.*

I like Oscar Wilde's:

> *To live is the rarest thing in the world. Most people exist, that is all.*

Aristotle, a teleologist (from the Greek telos, end or purpose), argues that all things strive to accomplish what they are meant to be. How well-done is it? How close to its best possibility is it? That determines how real it is. Natural to the teleologist: for each and every thing, there is a right way to be. Aristotle, the teleologist, asks: As the horseman must be expert at running the stables, and the home-keeper is expert at running the house, is there not an expertise on how man should live?

10. That is, individuals, civilizations too, must first determine proper methods for handling pressing practical affairs, both personally and culturally. Enroll Junior in shop class to learn by example the right way to do something. Junior will learn that doing it aright makes for a beautiful result.

> *Those who find beautiful meanings in beautiful things are the cultivated. For these there is hope. They are the elect to whom beautiful things mean only Beauty.*
>
> Oscar Wilde.

The masterpiece; *La Pieta*; Mary, at perfect peace, receiving the broken body of Christ; Michelangelo was twenty-three years old. The quarrymen showed him the huge—twice man-size—block of perfect marble; Michelangelo said *The David is in there, all I have to do is get rid of the debris.*

I like Oscar Wilde's:

> *We are all in the gutter, but some of us are looking up at the stars.*

Classic, Romantic

1. Today there is a cultural divide as to whether masculinity and femininity are natural and innate, or, well, contrived. The cultural Left thinks the distinction is artificial, intended by toxic masculinity to curtail the right of self-determination.

The Right says that God decided to make you man or woman, with the suggestion that it is a blasphemy to challenge divine decision. For secularists: *Don't mess with Mother Nature!* Perhaps being a man or a woman is the natural shape of your soul, the nucleus of your being.

I think so. The other side will say that genders are personae taken on by choice, the way Superman takes on his superpowers when he puts on his uniform and cape.

2. Is gender a personal preference? Like picking a meal or a mate? And should your choice be protected as a natural right? Here is a sort of illogical misuse of language. If the masculine/feminine is a made-up distinction and condemned by toxic masculinity, then *toxic masculinity* is a suspicious notion.

3. For secularists: male and female is not just a matter of genitalia but of personality. I do not think anyone denies that women, *by their nature*, harbor a maternal instinct. The male instinct, the *Zeus instinct*, is to provide and protect. If these instincts are securely in us and are self-defining, then they cannot be removed by altering genitalia.

4. The hard science of biology confirms that in all of us, men and women alike, the right hemisphere of every brain houses the decidedly romantic and, on the other side of our brain, classical facilities.

Seated in the left hemisphere, the classical side, is speech, language, logic and material organization by rules. That is, the left hemisphere of your brain, be you man or woman, is your classical side.

Seated in the right side of your brain: creativity, emotion, arousal. That is, the right hemisphere of your brain houses the romantic side of your soul, of your being. The hard science of biology supports the real presence in us of the classic/romantic distinction.

5. Not dirt, nothing inert and insignificant, but all serious things are made so by the gods who style them to be classically streamlined or romantically flushed. Know yourself better, know all things better, by recognizing and appreciating each thing's—and yours too—classical and romantic flavor, feature and character.

Sometimes examples are a better beginning. Punch up the Web and taste the flavor of the classical *Art Deco* and the romantic *Art Nouveau*.. The first three minutes of Tchaikovsky's Piano Concerto and its classically powerful percussion will make you stand up and salute. The next romantic minute of mellifluous melody will melt your heart. I prefer the Web available performance by perfectionist pianist, Lang Lang.

6. The romance languages know that a thing's proper name must include its gender. **Le** *soleil,* French for the *masculine* Sun; **la** *lune,* the feminine moon. The Sun, the name of the powerful controlling light source for life, a classical masculinity allowing the Earth to continue as the abode for life. Moonlight caresses and comforts the Earth with her delicate, seductive light play.

Call it male, masculine, or classical; call it female, feminine, or romantic; the classical/romantic distinction colors, flavors, imbues all things with this theme of essential reality. Know better the nature of things when you know them to be the forcefully and handsomely streamlined Apollonian or the passionately pretty, arousable Dionysian.

7. Historical introduction to the personality defining classic vs. romantic: Apollonian mathematical analysis and Dionysian musical ecstasy. The god Zeus, ruler of Olympus, had two sons: demure, elegant, formal, *classical* Apollo, *the rational*, and his devilish brother, besotted with drink, the *romantic* Dionysus, *the emotional.*

> *But the Gods, taking pity on mankind, born to work, laid down the succession of recurring Feasts to restore them from their fatigue, and gave them the muses, and Apollo their leader, and Dionysus, as companions in their Feasts, so that nourishing themselves in festive companionship with the Gods, they should again stand straight and erect.*
>
> Attributed to Plato; quoted in *Leisure; The Basis of Culture* by Joseph Pieper.

Greek mythology is no childish fairytale, but profound insight into the human condition with use of dramatic allegory. The sons of Zeus, masculine Apollo and romantic Dionysus, are the Adam and Eve of Zeus' garden. Perhaps the masculine and romantic are the most poignant moments and most telling characteristics of human personality.

> *The Gods, according to Nietzsche, in "The Birth of Tragedy," knew very well that life is terrible, inexplicable, dangerous. But though they were alive to the real character of the nature of the world and of human life, they did not surrender to pessimism by turning their backs on life. What they did was to transmute the world and human life through the medium of art. And they then were able to say yes to the world as an aesthetic phenomenon. There were, however, two ways of doing this, corresponding respectively to the Dionysian or Apollonian attitudes or mentalities*

> *... the ideal world of form and beauty, this is the Apollonian way ... The other possibility is that of triumphantly affirming and embracing existence in all its darkness and horror. Is the Dionysian attitude, and its typical art forms are tragedy and music.*
>
> Fr. Copleston, "Nietzsche" in The History of Philosophy, Vol. 7.

8. A new way to better know your world: Is the dynamic reality of everything flavored and better revealed through the ambiance and ambivalence of its classically masculine and romantically feminine traits?

For anything and everything of significance to the human condition: Compare its physical state, so classically described by the senses and verifiable as a matter of fact, with the romance of what would bring it to a self-loving ecstatic deliciousness.

Take anything, and compare it, on the on the one hand, with its classical factual description, under the watchful empiricist eye, with, on the other hand, what brings it to a rhapsodic thrill, as yearns the romantic rationalist.

9. A nice opening to a better understanding of our historical periods:

The Classical Age of Reason, the Enlightenment, circa the 1700s; the founding and progress of modern science. Is anything more classical than the pursuit of objective truth? The new science is pursued with confidence and conviction that all mysteries that matter will unravel by the power of clear and distinct observation together with unprejudiced reason. The world will be forced to yield its secrets.

Famed poet Alexander Pope said of Newton:

> *In the Beginning all was night; God said* **Let Newton Be** *and all was light.*

During this century of science, as questions are answered, and more difficult questions are discovered and pursued, there is no progress in questions of the human heart and soul. After a century of classical scientific effort, it is realized: *What sort of man could love a mathematical formula or a technological device?*

The romantic rebellion of the 1800s is a turn to desire and passion, a love affair with loveliness and the natural. It came to be appreciated that scientific truth stays a distance away from immediate experience and can never satisfy our lust for the lushness of the lived world.

To be sure, science discovers a world, but not the world of lived experience. Let's have the vivid truth of *Lebenswelt*, the immediacy of the *world-as-lived*. Bored and tired with the *noble achiever*, the romantic admires the *noble savage*. Never mind that the primitive is uncivilized.

Belief, powered by objective truth, was attempted in the Enlightenment and found wanting. Let's have the truth of belief powered, not by cold logic, but by hot, feisty, if hasty, commitment to whatever arouses the passions.

The nineteenth-century romantic was little aware of the coming twentieth-century classical development of *belief systems*, and the founding of *group-think*. *Group-think*: What does that even mean?

Invigorated by the Industrial Revolution, the 1900s is fascinated with and captured by gadgets and technology, restricts and reduces knowledge to the facts, all the facts and only the facts. As though by herding together all the disparate facts they will somehow coalesce into a meaningful structure. Test question: Is this romantic or classical?

10. From Bertrand Russell's *A History of Western Philosophy*:

The romantic movement is characterized, as a whole, by the substitution of aesthetic for utilitarian standards. The earth-worm is useful, but not beautiful, the tiger is beautiful, but not useful. Darwin (who was not a romantic) praised the earth-worm; Blake praised the tiger.

A taste of Nietzsche, exemplar of the romantic:

Without music, life would be a mistake.

Ah, women. They make the highs higher and the lows more frequent.

We have art in order not to die from the truth.

I would believe only in a God that knows how to Dance.

There are no facts, only interpretations.

Character

1. I know what you will think if I tell you that the ancient Greeks were a *serious* people. *Were not the Egyptians and the Chinese serious people?*

To be(come) Egyptian or Chinese is to be born into a cookie-cutter shaping that forms you to be a proper Egyptian or properly Chinese. You are pre-determined by an irresistible authoritarian power and so kowtow to unbendable rule and control demanded by pharaoh and emperor. The Greeks were born into a question: *What can you—will you—achieve?*

The Greeks were the first *citizens*. To be a citizen of Athens, a self-determining, democratic, city-state, it is demanded that you be(come) all that you can be. For example, it is required that you speak your mind on issues that will be decided by citizen contribution, argument and analysis and majority vote. The Greeks invented the notion that we are self-responsible individuals with deep appreciation for excellence in both ourselves and our fellows.

Much later, English Enlightenment leader, John Locke will argue that the definition of legitimate government is measured by the degree to which its power is derived from the consent of the governed. Locke's argument begins in ancient Athens.

2. I know what you are thinking. Why is this so momentous achievement by the Greeks and no other ancients? The answer is so mundane it surprises:

Civilization—all civilizations—begin as a thoroughly agricultural phenomenon. Only a well-fed exploding population can be organized to build Pharaoh's pyramids and the emperor's Great Wall. But our Western civilization, made by a hardy people, migrating down the Greek peninsula, had no agricultural plenitude. This civilization—our civilization—depended on trade and business to support survival.

Masters of the oceans, the Greeks explored all corners of the known world and analyzed every new thing they found. They traded and investigated from the English islands to as far away as China. Greek olive oil was the prized international commodity of the ancient world and this they traded for most of the grain they needed to survive.

Only hardy olives and grapes are natural and native to Greece. Other than these, only scrubs cling to life in a clayed and rocky soil with hardly a plateau to be seen. The Greeks were the sole ancient civilization with no vast agricultural abundance to meet the demands of brute physical survival. If democracy were to happen anywhere, it must be here, by self-determining men where survival requires the self-achievement and creative contribution of each individual. That is, of each citizen.

Greece is indeed a hard land, capable of maintaining only a small population, but if this population faces its tasks with decision, it will reap its rewards. ... Such a land demands that its inhabitants be tough, active, enterprising and intelligent. ... Men living in such circumstances needed more ... unflagging industry, careful foresight, skill ... The handling of ships demands quickness of eye and hand, agility and lightness of movement, unrestingly diligence, and rapidity of decision. Geographical

> *circumstance formed the Greek character by forcing it to make the most of its natural aptitudes ...*
>
> C. M. Bowra, *The Greek Experience.*

3. The Greeks know that life is hard. For most peoples, nothing to do but endure it. For the Greeks, success in life required the industry and self-realization that builds character rather than willing conformity to authority, convention, and custom.

Life is very hard; what to do about that? The Greeks invented art; bringing the delicious realization that aesthetics is the most promising source to test the meaning of life by manifesting the meaning of humanity in comedy and tragedy.

That marvelous Greek insight: the purpose of life is to pursue the exquisite, the excellent, the sublime; all else is mundane and unworthy of a life lived well. The mantra that haunts our Western understanding: *the unexamined life is not worth living.* To understand life and its uniquely human demands, the Greeks emphasized the classic and the romantic modes of human achievement.

> ***The Greeks, according to Nietzsche in* Birth of Tragedy, *knew very well that life is terrible, inexplicable, dangerous. But though they were alive to the real character of the nature of the world and of human life, they did not surrender to pessimism by turning their backs on life ...There were, however, two ways of doing this, corresponding respectively to the Dionysian and Apollonian Attitudes or mentalities. ...The ideal world of form and beauty, this is the Apollonian way. ... The other possibility is that of triumphantly affirming and embracing existence in all its darkness and horror. This is the Dionysian attitude and its typical art forms are tragedy and music. And they then were able to say yes to the world as an aesthetic medium of art.***

Fr. Frederick Copleston, "Nietzsche," A History of Philosophy, Vol. 7.

4. Ordinary life is unscrupulous and inconsequential in its indecisive innocence. The trouble with life lived innocently is that it is conventional, mundane, mediocre and of course, unsatisfying. It is the life of children and beasts.

The terrible tragedy (yes, this is a romantic view) of human life: either surrender to innocence, to the conventional and the ordinary or shoulder human responsibility. Meet the demand to become serious despite the mundanity of physical existence and pressure to conform to convention. Achieve a serious life or remain innocent. Build character.

For all other peoples, life is by diktat of authority commanded from on high. To be Greek is to ask *how to be*, and to be free to be(come) what you will be(come) by transcending the physically random circumstance of factual existence.

5. The beast must, and most people, too, surrender to nature (structural in heritance) and nurture (environmental pressure). But we are the only creature capable of transcending physical and environmental determination, to not only be but to be(come). Socrates instructs on how to do it; begin here, with the decision that the unexamined life is not worth living.

We, the only creatures responsible to make ourselves to be; seriously, how to become a person of character. What to do about the blemish of existence; we, the only creatures that know about it. That, dear reader, is the purpose of, and need for, art.

The challenge is awful. Here's what to do. The person of character will relish the challenge, make it their own with a life lived in appreciation of the comic and the tragic, the romantic and the classical. How else – where else – to find the excellent and the exquisite?

That's the ancient Greek instruction with their elaborate tales of Apollo and Dionysius, the sons of Zeus.

Again:

> *The ideal world of form and beauty, this is the Apollonian way. ... The other possibility is that of triumphantly affirming and embracing existence in all its darkness and horror. This is the Dionysian attitude and its typical art forms are tragedy and music. And they then were able to say yes to the world as an aesthetic medium of art.*

Fr. Frederick Copleston, "Nietzsche," A History of Philosophy, Vol. 7.

A Serious Person

1. In the movie blockbuster, *The Godfather*, Marlon Brando portrays a dark but very serious person. Everything decided by the master of the Corleone crime family has far-reaching consequence. Whether or not we approve of him, we are fascinated. The Godfather is more powerful than local or federal authority, and can, at will, wreak havoc on his enemies, all within a moral code to which he is more loyal than the average American is to our Constitution. Indeed, his sense of right and wrong dominates all he does.

One of his constituents, the local baker, appeals to the Godfather to exact revenge upon his daughter's rapists who had been found innocent by the court. The Godfather deploys the correct moral tone of his empire. The baker wants the rapists killed:

I ask you for justice.

The Godfather: *That is not justice; your daughter is still alive.*

The baker: *They can suffer then, as she suffers. How much shall I pay you?*

The Godfather: *Had you come to me in friendship, then this scum that ruined your daughter would be suffering this very day. And that by chance if an honest man such as yourself should make enemies, then they would become my enemies. And then they would fear you.*

The baker: *Be my friend ... Godfather?*

The Godfather: *Good! Accept this justice as a gift on my daughter's wedding day.*

The Godfather, to his consiglieri (don't you love that word?) after the baker leaves the room: *Give this to, ah, Clemenza. I want reliable people; people that aren't gonna be carried away. I mean, we're not murderers.*

The topic is justice, as in Plato's Republic. Only we, no other creature, measure the meaning of life on the scales of justice. The Constitution of the United States does; so does the Corleone crime family. To be sure, the Don's rules are not our rules, but we cannot help but be tantalized and transfixed by the brilliant world-shaking display of how serious a person is the Godfather and his Achilles-sized utter commitment to the rules of life as he sees it.

2. This morality tale is told by persons as serious and consequential in their effect on the world they inhabit as Grecian Olympic heroes. Vito Corleone versus his mafia competitors is like Achilles versus Hector. We are fascinated by valiant giants battling with their all to protect and promote the rules of serious human life—permeated as is human life by we-all-make-our-own-hell strife.

We are fascinated by the tale of the Godfather because, whatever we think of the merits of his code of conduct, we know that only humans can become persons by adopting a code of conduct, even if that code can lead us into tragedy. All existence is prone to catastrophe; you and I are the only creatures able and liable to make our own hell—be(come) tragic victims. The Greeks called it *hubris*.

Only you and I can be, well, insolent—and arrogant—indulging our tendency (as philosopher Martin Heidegger says) to step outside ourselves and reach beyond ourselves. You and I are the only creatures capable of breaking the restraints of convention, of reaching beyond the usual and the mundane. Yes, we are the only creatures capable of temperance and reason. But, too, of their opposites.

Is the Godfather sinful? I suppose so. But the point is we are the only creatures capable of sin, of hubris. That defines us. All others are innocent.

3. I know what you are thinking ... *But this is a story of evil; the Godfather is not a good man. He breaks the law, commits heinous crimes. He is a sociopath ready to flaunt the norms of civil society and follow only his own rules.* Oh, yes. I understand your comment and I want to ask: *Do you claim to know what makes a good man?* Do you *follow the norms of civil society* because you admire them? Or because, well, you don't want any trouble?

What makes a man more fully human? What makes a man a good man? Does it begin with he does not break the law, and is, therefore, good? Or, rather, is it not the case that laws seek to control behavior but cannot make men good, or better...or serious?

What makes a man a good man? Perhaps the mark of a good man is not by some measure of *goodness*. Not by a set of Aristotelian virtues (*nothing in excess, all in moderation*), or rules defined by reason (such as Kant's Categorical Imperative, *Do to others as you would have them do to you*) or by the ever so popular utilitarian *Do that which enhances the most happiness and pleasure and the least discomfort*.

Perhaps the mark of a good man is not by some measure of *goodness*, but of commitment (no matter the price) and loyalty to whatever moral code we adopt. Ergo, the Godfather.

4. Do we follow the rules because we want to be good or because we want to avoid recrimination? Obeying the law is easier, an inculcated habit like tying shoelaces, it is what we all do. Are we aware of why

we do it? Do we do what we do by deliberation and decision, or mechanically, by convention and custom? Are we autonomous or are we herd-driven to simple habitual behavior?

We ordinary folk follow the law...why? Because laws are just and we are eager to preserve the civil order or because we are shamed into obedience and not serious enough to pay the fine or go to jail?

Do we obey the law for any reason more serious than innocent habit? As you are considering, think of this. Everything he does has large consequence; we are in awe of the godfather's awful seriousness. And think of this: Superman gives the bad guys a quick and final kibosh and is unfettered by due process. That doesn't bother us at all.

5. Wait. Isn't everyone, seriously, a person? Think of a new baby elephant and it would be correct to say, *That's an elephant, fully constituted, completely real.* But can we say of a newly born human, *That's a person?* Is a newborn a person? Seriously, a person? A serious person? Or only *potentially* a serious person? From birth, elephants live as elephants, some might say more successfully, and with no extra effort needed, than we ourselves achieve personhood. But one thing the elephant cannot do is say what is an elephant.

To ask, *What is an elephant?* or, *Who and what am I?* ... Only you and I can do that. And this we must, if we are to become persons. But the newborn human child, like the mature elephant, does not know what the question means. Correct?

6. What is unique and defining of us as persons? What distinguishes us from all other creatures? Only we can speak for the elephant, and too, for ourselves. I think the world waits for us to speak for it. Too romantic a notion?

There is history to the question, *what makes us to be human?* Some answers have been religious, uniquely gifted by God with not only sensibility, but reason, self-reflective deliberation, and free will. Some answers are more descriptive and scientific, others more philosophical.

Behaviorist social science focuses on efficient and facile opposing thumbs. That tool-using defines us had to be given with the discovery of adept tool-users throughout the animal kingdom.

Animal behaviorists thought they had determined the elements of our definition as social cementing by communication and relationship. But revolutionary linguist Noam Chomsky convinced us that language developed in man, not primarily as a communicative device, but as a vehicle for this unique human capacity: creative rational thought.

Philosophically speaking, I prefer, *What makes us to be persons?* rather than the more scientifically popular (examine the behavior), *How are we persons?* Behaviorists think that humanness suggests something factual, informational and physically circumstantial, descriptive of the physical structure of homo sapiens. This does not satisfy my need to know who and what I am.

I am asking for something other, something more, than a physical description. What it means to be Homo sapiens is a matter of fact. What it means to be a person is not.

7. My inquiry: *What* is a person, *seriously?* This question is not satisfiable with a description of our physical make-up, of how we look and how the architecture of our physical structure works. The behaviorists have instructed us that we are another species that cement social relationship with messaging and communication and use tools. This will explain what is, and how is, a monkey and an elephant, and, too, how we endure mundane life, but cannot begin to explore what it means—seriously—to be a person.

I am convinced: the first thing to know about us is that we are the only beings responsible to make ourselves to be, to become, by our own self-responsible achievement, the promise of our self-achieving essential nature contained in our potential. I call that *serious* life. Or, so sad, so pervasive, so often we settle for the ordinary and unserious, for the life of the beast, remaining content with the inconsequential.

Physical description does well enough for the monkey and elephant. Bless the social sciences, psychology and sociology and anthropology; they work so hard to model our understanding of ourselves simply and mechanically on animal-like instinct and behavior; as though we are conditioned by habit to unthinking response, like the flower that cannot help but grow to its light source.

Serious study concentrates on the most achieved of us. To know ourselves, we need to understand our essential reality, the depth and height of our potential. To know ourselves, it is not enough to describe how we happen to be, we must explore what each of us might become. Let us look at the most ideal examples of what it means to be a person, and leave studies of the average, the ordinary, the run of the mill, yes, the inconsequential, to the social sciences.

8. Let us look at Achilles, Vito Corleone, Superman, the icons that Nietzsche called the *Übermensch*, the more-than-man. What I have called the serious man. For philosopher Martin Heidegger, Nietzsche's Übermensch is the very meaning of man, the creature that is what he is only when he strives to surpass himself.

Socrates' injunction for the serious life: *the unexamined life is not worth living.* Examine what? Resist the temptation to surrender to easy inconsequential happenstance. Unexamined, life is not lived, but endured. Of all creatures, only you can examine, choose, and decide to be serious.

9. Un-serious is the soul with no center, bending to the winds of fashion. Un-serious souls can fall to the wiles of Satan. Uncentered

souls are innocent, so better beware Beelzebub. Let us say it again. Unserious souls lack a central core of commitment and loyalty to belief that validates our sense of worthiness and self-respect.

I Feel Like ...

I feel like ... as though what and how I feel determines what is true *... for me!*

I feel like ... a very clever use of language to camouflage our surrender to stupidity.

I feel like ... what?

I am a good person, so if it pleases me it must be good.

Thoughts I like are true because, well, I like them.

The local team deserves our support because that is neighborly ... and neighborliness is good.

Do we disagree about something? Not good. Agreement brings harmony ... and harmony is good.

Is what you find emotionally satisfying an acceptable test for truth ... an acceptable test for what you believe?

Nice question: *What persuades you?* Does how you feel about something persuade you to the truth about it? Do you allow your feeling to render what you believe believable, and therefore, emotionally acceptable, or even emotionally irresistible? Do you think that what is emotionally satisfying is a good test for truth, a good test for what to believe?

And what more is there to *truth* than your commitment to a point of view ... correct? What point of view? Starting with Mommy, people you know will provide that for you.

It's human nature. You are a chip off the old block, you must believe as do your friends, else you won't have any.

1. Squarely old-fashioned and coolly postmodern, such different expectations of how to experience our world. Marshall McLuhan's (*The Medium is the Message*) grand insight into our postmodern era: Old-fashioned *square* people are *content-oriented*, analyzing with philosophy and science the degree of objectivity that mark and measure the reality of the things we encounter in our experience of the world.

Contemporary cool people do not encounter and analyze their world; they participate in it. They do not seek to explain the world, but rather to explore how it *feels*.

This is a contemporary (post-World War II) move away from the traditional West that wants to *understand*, and for millennia, put the world to a scientific and philosophical analysis. This is a postmodern wink at the East that thinks the world is authentically available to us only through our active participation in it—and with it—and immediately. How romantic: only intimacy and commitment count. No feeling more profound and compelling than *authenticity*. But no one has told me what that means.

McLuhan notes that *disinterested* used to mean unbiased and estimated with fair-minded objectivity. Now, postmodernly, *disinterested* means I am only interested in how I feel about things.

2. Postmodernism is a *classical* redux. Available to us is only what can be empirically detected, physically described, and factually verified. Some say that soon, the only world that entices will be the virtual

world, a computer-generated environment that fools the senses, looks, feels, sounds, tastes and smells, with themes and things and people, technically transcending all that is natural, and all that is real. *Un-real* is okay if it titillates and tickles my fancy and it is fun to participate in imaginaries.

The *romantic* edge of postmodernism: The only reality that makes sense to us is the one we make up in our own subjective, idiosyncratic, private, mind-altered imagination.

Appeal by emotion over logically defended persuasion: If it feels good, believe it, take it, live it. If you can imagine it, try it; *expand consciousness* to all possibilities. All possibilities are equally good. *Good* means they are new and invite a look-see. Every possible new experience is exciting and rewarding just because it is new. What is worthwhile, and yes, worth our while, other than new experience?

3. Good and evil defy both physical description and technical systems analysis. Good and evil and the beautiful and the ugly are personal whims, sentiments. The exquisite and the sublime are a bridge too far for life lived for experience sake. *Technical systems analysis*, with manipulating tools like artificial intelligence, enhance computer-constructed milieus that replace and transcend the natural order with more pleasing and exciting artificial environments.

Philosophy, poetry, history, art and the hopes of classical science from the mid-1600s to the mid-1900s are the has-beens of the classical-romantic struggle to apprehend, intend, and appreciate the essentials of reality.

Truth, value, ethics, beauty, the noble, all reach for the sublime, all deserve our sympathetic encounter, respect and appreciation as well as our allegiance and advocacy. But they have become childish playthings —of no moment or consequence for postmodern man.

The new Sermon on the Mount: No advocacy or self-sacrifice is advisable, needed, or necessary. The current fashion: *be comfortable*. Why suffer discomfort? If it *feels* right, then, it must *be* right.

Objective truth has fallen out of reach and is replaced with subjective and private phantasmagorias. The medium has become the message.

4. New to philosophy and eager for a definition, or at least a hint on how to begin, we wonder … philosophy is about … what? Let us look first at what philosophy does so that we can begin to say what it is.

Philosophy points to three terrible errors to which we are prone in our pre-philosophical, and post-philosophical lives.

We think:

i. The primary purpose of language is *communication*, to deliver messages. Language is but a tool, used by and useful to man and beast alike. For both man and beast, communication makes personal relationship and social cohesion possible. Nothing is so consequential for social cultural formation as communication and relationship. Ask any social scientist, psychologist to sociologist.

ii. *The world is as it appears*, offering itself up to eye and ear so that we can find out how we feel about things. The empirical physical (that's redundant) senses are our only immediate, direct, uninterruptible contact and encounter with our world. We think the senses make the world ours. This view is called *naïve realism*.

The business of living is to practice a fine-honed, sharp-edged commonsense guide to winning, in all practical matters. The *good life* is yours if you work hard and make a smiley-faced acknowledgement to all expectations. If you are clever, you might not even have to work hard.

We model our understanding of humanness on animal behavior. Man and beast, both in like manner, make their way, cut their path, with communication delivering the messages which form social cooperation. Life is a game, and the point is to win ... win what? Social success that brings with it, of course, financial and political first place prizes.

iii. *Truth is relative.* To ... what? To how you happen to feel about things! *Psychologism* speaks the language of *true to him, her, or them*. *Psychologism* is the terrible logical error that makes truth a function of the mental event that expresses a truth. Those suffering from psychologism are prone to say *true to him, her, them*. Clear to every straight thinker, objective truth is separate and distinct from the subjective act of expressing it.

5. Philosophy rudely intrudes into this Dale Carnegie-esque, commonsensy, easy, pleasingly smug, self-satisfying view.

Socrates is horrified by the description above, apt to his time, two thousand years ago. Ancient Greek uses the word, *doxa*, for feelings and appearances, for do-as-you-feel and all that is utterly subjective and disconnected from universal, essential, necessary truth.

Rude, bothersome and annoying, Socrates shames his fellow Athenians into to defending the so subjective, smug, egocentric and self-satisfying relativism described above. So bitter the debate, believe it or not, they executed him. Socrates, champion and martyr for the dictum: **The unexamined life is not worth living**.

Examine ... what? The Sophists (from which we get our *sophisticated*) of Socrates' time, as well as today's postmoderns, sadly evade and avoid the language uniquely defining what it means to be a person, and not an innocent, pre-determined by nature and nurture, as are all other animals.

6. The more old-fashioned, conservative and traditional expectation: The world presents itself as an interconnected bundle of content, non-self-explanatory, challenging our understanding, with a meaning and significance to be deciphered. Here the urge to science and philosophy. Let us render intelligible the apparent chaos of sensed experience; knowledge is power and science will unravel our perplexities.

Enthusiasts of both the classical, empiricist English Enlightenment and the romantic and rational continental Age of Reason, the intelligentsia on both sides of the English Channel, on both the left and the right of Europe, were certain the world was about to yield up her secrets to scientific and philosophical enquiry.

Since the eighteenth-century English-speaking Enlightenment, and the continental Age of Reason, experience of the world was to be analyzed and rendered understandable by application of the unique human intellect to unravel the chaotic appearance the world makes to our senses.

But progress was slow. So comes the romantic rebellion beginning with Immanuel Kant. It, too, loses its mojo. First science set about to establish certain-to-be-achieved objective truth. Then came the ecstatic appreciation of the beautiful and the sublime.

A century and a half of Empiricism, Rationalism, of Classicism and its counterpoint, Romanticism, and European life finds little improvement. Perhaps the hope was vain. Enter our postmodern age beginning at the end of World War II as we continue to fail at finding solutions to our vexations.

7. Traditionally philosophy is located in the more old-fashioned, conservative expectation: If we well enough understand our questions, then answers will be forth coming. Our new postmodern world has no patience for the old-fashioned, painstaking scientific and philosophical analysis.

Science brought us the atom bomb; we've moved from Beethoven to rap; no need to include Michelangelo in art books. But everyone can count on life's meaning in personal experience, bathing in the pool of authenticity, and commitment for commitment's sake.

8. From 1650 to 1800, a century-and-a-half of enlightenment, of faith in and commitment to *progress:* The so hopeful 1700s makes mighty strides towards liberty in the American, and then, in the increasing horrible stages of the French revolution.

A century-and-a-half of enlightenment, of faith and a commitment to *progress* defines enlightenment in the West. The so hopeful 1700s makes mighty strides, revolutionary leaps to liberty. The French taste sweet liberty as they partner with the American colonies and then try it on for themselves.

The incredible American Revolution was an impossible win by sheer determination over the world's mightiest and most invincible military power. Then, alas, a false step by romantic French and her terrible guillotine.

The French Revolution takes a dreadful turn, veering left, putting Frenchmen at the mercy of basest instincts. In the early nineteenth century Europe turns left to the Romantic Movement, to a search for meaning-as-sentiment, that is, well, emotional politics-by-feeling, emphasizing the priority of community over the individual, community welfare over individual rights and over the protection of property.

Very un-French, but very American: Only limited government can and will protect and promote an individual's right to life, liberty and the pursuit of happiness. In France, not science, but affection, becomes the hope for mankind's success. Revolutionary France doesn't quite know how to shoulder the classical themes of *liberté* and *égalité,* but is romantically enthused by and committed to *fraternité.* To paraphrase

Mr. Spock of *Star Trek*: *The good of the many out-weigh the good of the individual.*

For those of improper sentiment: Bring them to the guillotine.

Continental Europe in the 1800s is ignited by the passions. From the eighteenth-century's logical analysis, cold science, and a determined respect for the rights of the individual begins movement to the hot, enchanting, and exciting nineteenth century. Now comes Jean-Jacques Rousseau and the French lurch to the left. Alas, the French march to communal-ism and the individual losses his political standing.

When President Nixon spoke with leaders of Communist China, he asked Mao's right-hand man, Zhou Enlai, if Zhou thought the French revolution was successful. Remarkably, revealingly and presciently Zhou replied, *We do not yet know.*

The Declaration of the Rights of Man (France's revolutionary founding document) like the Americans they supported with ship, soldier and gun, declares for liberty and equality, but—here's the French romantic twist—only if the demands of the commune, of fraternité, are met.

The American fight was for life, liberty and the pursuit of happiness, the inherent rights of the individual. The French champion life, liberty, and *fraternité*. That is, in the French romantic view, our primary responsibility is for one another.

9. Recently, many of us have taken to what we think is the Eastern view … the world is only available to us through direct and immediate experience and by our active participation in it and with it. We used to wrap our minds around it; now we wrap our arms around the world, let it feel our heartbeat, and read haiku.

No longer is education an instruction through which to *learn*. Now, education is, well, un-goaled other than to have an educational *experience*.

The new clarion call: *Get in touch with feelings, yours and everyone else's.* We strive for an utterly non-judgmental encounter with as many things as possible, equally things of men and things of mud. *Things of evil?* Yes, those too.

Postmodernism, a *classical* redux: Experience is delimited to only what can be immediately encountered, sensibly described, empirically detected, and factually verified. Some say that soon, the only world we will permit ourselves will be the virtual world, AI constructed, technically transcending all that is natural.

The only questions we will pursue will be those to which we bring pre-determined virtual answers.

The *romantic* edge of postmodernism: The only reality that makes sense to us is the one we make up in our own subjective, idiosyncratic, private, mind-altered imagination. Objective truth has fallen out of reach and has been replaced with subjective and private phantasmagorias.

The medium has become the message; Marshall McLuhan ... call your office.

10. Here's how far it has gone. Students engage college-level material with ... *I feel that ... I agree with ... I like*, but with little sense of whether or not what they like, or dislike, rests on any solid evidence or analysis.

Registering a *like* on Facebook has replaced critical thinking, and counts as a student learning exercise ... uh, a *learning experience.* Learning once meant *master the material,* now learning means *experience it.*

11. Philosophy, poetry, history, art, and the hopes of classical science, too, are the has-beens of the classical/romantic struggle of the 1700s. They have been relegated to the historical dustbin. Objective truth, value, ethics, beauty, the novel, that which deserves our respect and

appreciation, allegiance and advocacy including the reach for the sublime are now childish playthings of no moment for postmodern man.

12. Far away, long ago, Shakespeare's light on life: *All the world's a stage, we are but players.* Now, five hundred years later, as our postmodern classical edge would have it, intelligibility is reduced and limited to a technical representation of reality. Life reduced to team-punk, illusion speaks louder than words, not worth one snapshot. Personal experience is more valuable ... uh, exciting ... than demonstrated objective truth.

Our postmodern romantic edge: *It is prima facie true, I cannot escape myself and my subjective awareness. True* means *true-to-me. It counts* means *it counts-for-me.* Beauty is, of course, in the eye of the beholder, and means *I like it.*

Aesthetically valuable means it happens to attract my notice, and is, therefore, worthy of a glance ... *by me.* You are isolate in your own monad; we monads can know one another only formally, by a pre-established harmony that forbids any intense intimacy.

Worthy means it attracts me and my esteem. If what is estimable to you happens to strike you differently from the way it strikes me ... Hey! All is by personal estimate and *different strokes for different folks.*

The only thing we need agree on is that we be tolerant of each other's idiosyncratic peculiarities. Virtue is achieved by a Buddha-like non-judgmental tolerance—even of crap. So postmodern!

The only sin is narrow-minded and damnable judgementalism. The postmodern test of truth: intuitive comfort. If it feels good: believe it; do it; permit it; advocate it—but only to those to whom it also feels good ... because we are tolerant of all sensibilities.

13. Relativism rules: worthy means *worthy-to-me* and *worthy-to-you*. What's *worthy-to-you* and *worthy-to-me* may be very different. Our beliefs may contradict, but we will applaud commitment to any belief whatsoever.

In the postmodern world no one is incorrect, we are all monads, imprisoned in the jail of our own self-reflective awareness. It is true that we believe so-and-so and such-and-such, therefore what we believe is true ... *for us*. We have no need for the truth to go further than that. Now all objective universal standards are bigotries. Consensus brings harmony; harmony is the highest good, Cicero's *Summum Bonum*.

Persuasion

What persuades you?

1. To find out what sort of person you are, should you examine your likes, beliefs, and attitudes? Or should you examine what persuades you to those beliefs and makes attractive those likes and attitudes?

For all too many of us, persuasion is geographic. I live in Colorado and everyone I know who cares, roots for the Broncos. As a boy in New York, I remember the diatribe recounting the merits of the Brooklyn Dodgers versus the New York Yankees. We Brooklynites loved *dem bums*, and hoity-toity Manhattanites admired the sophisticated pin-striped Bronx Bombers, who had plenty of money to buy talent.

We Brooklynites were persuaded as a matter of the heart—*Just you wait till next year!* What persuaded Yankee fans? Don't know. But I am sure that these fans (short for *fanatics*)—were driven to emote their Brooklyn-ese romanticism and Manhattan-ese classicism. After all, all the important museums are in Manhattan. And what is more classical than Yankee pinstripes and unparalleled success on the diamond? But, the underdog Brooklyn Bums had a hold on our hearts.

I like the question: Do you allow yourself to be defined by your geographic location, by the local gang of fanatics? Does where you live determine who and what you are? Should you continue to accept that?

Is this not prejudice? Is there anything more corrosive to the soul than the demands of the local gang?

2. It's a particular sort of evil to think our likes and beliefs are true or recommendable just because we like them, or because someone else, or lots of our fellows, or everyone around us, likes them. An example of the latter is the so pervasive geographic prejudice described above. And the devil is delighted with our fanaticism. He knows that many of us would sell our soul to help the local team, whoever the hell they are.

Here's an example of another sort of geographic prejudice. Almost ninety percent of New York City voters, and, too, citizens of Washington, DC, pull the lever for the Democratic Party. Not so in Idaho. You might think there is something in the air on the American east coast.

This sort of blind fealty denies the stalwart tradition of American pride in individualism and respect for critical thinking. I suggest this is another sort of geographical compulsion ... *All my friends and neighbors think and vote this way.*

3. Do you have a soul? I think you do. If you have not met it yet, here's why. We are so busy with the common sense demands of day-in and day-out living. We are a practical people - we get things done! What serves personal and social and financial success is the reason to work, the reason to live, and the reason to believe as we do.

We are a practical people—success is the goal. But although busy pursuing our life goals, we must attend to our needs, that is to say, our frailties. With fine-honed common sense we mean to deal with the blemish of existence ...

... The Blemish of Existence! Existing things get bumped and bruised, then age, rot and die. If it exists, then it is constantly changing, searching for a better way to deal with the hardships of surviving the challenges of the harsh and demanding physical world.

4. To deal with life, God gave no creature other than man free will, reason, and a self-reflective sense of right and wrong. Only man can distinguish what is necessary from happenstance, the excellent from the ordinary, the exquisite from the mundane. The devil endowed us with common sense. Too many of us are too ready to sell our soul to get ahead. To that end we value common sense above all other virtues.

Common sense is obsessed not with what *is* better but with what *works* better. From the devil, common sense focuses on the lived-world (Germans have a tastier *Lebenswelt*) and disdains as irrelevant what is necessarily true, exquisitely uncommon, objectively beautiful, and sublime. The devil smirks. The Good has been demoted in favor of Personal Benefit.

Stalwart Socrates stood against this devilish common sense. Socrates versus the Sophists: Western Civilization begins with this furious debate between Socrates and the common-sensors of his day.

5. There is a two-fold ambiguity concerning what is *common* (lowest common denominator, or, so undeniable as to be adopted by all reasonable people) and the *sense* (or *sensibleness*) of common sense.

The devil's *common* sense is of this *commonality*: the lowest common denominator. And by *sensibility*, the devil wants us to restrict our deliberations and considerations to fact, to haphazard circumstance, to the physical senses of eye and ear, to *information*.

The devil lures us to settle for the easy, seductively vivid and vivacious, helplessly received appearance of things. He would have us shy away from what is hidden behind appearance and more difficult to apprehend. He would make us shy away from what is necessarily true, excellent, exquisite, beautiful and sublime.

Sense and sensibility: what ambiguity! The devil prefers *sense* in the sense of sense data, information we passively receive by eye and ear. On the other hand, there is the more divine *sense* of sensibility, as in the intelligibility that requires, depends on and waits for the proactive engine of the understanding.

6. This distinction between sense and sensibility is reflected in a similar ambiguity concerning language. Language is a powerful thing, but not when it is just delivering a message. That is language as communication, used by both man and monkey, to receive and deliver messages. But there is a uniquely human critical and creative thought that has only human language as its medium and condition of possibility.

To speak the truth, appreciate the exquisite, distinguish the necessary from the accidental, pledge support for the noble and the just … only man can do that. To do that requires a vehicle, and the only vehicle that can do that: language.

7. J'accuse! Yes, dear reader, I accuse us of taking this devil path of obsession with information. A careful reflection and we will realize that it is not true that all truth is factual; what is significant in human life is what can be established as necessary and undeniable.

On the other hand, all facts are description of happenstance, of what *happens* to be taking place. The devil convinces us to value facts over value, information over necessity, on the pretense that information informs because it states what could be—in other circumstances—other than it happens to be. But happenstance is not the stuff of necessity, what we need if are really to know about the nature of reality.

That we are able to know what *must* be the case, and that we are able to distinguish what must be from what happens to be: that reveals what it means to be a person. No other creature can do that. It is the devil's business, though, to raise to significance information above such necessary truth as value and beauty, the divine and the exquisite.

The devil giggles while he persuades us that information is substantial, not just circumstantial and casual happenstance. The devil has his arm around our shoulder, confident of winning our soul as we preen with pride that we are convinced by the facts and take care of life with the precepts of common sense demoting the Good and the Beautiful to insubstantial opinion.

8. My two heroes, Thomas Paine and John Locke, offer political analysis not diluted by mundane facts, not stultified by mere information, but by the proper understanding of the facts, and the very uncommon American Revolutionary understanding of citizenship.

Paine's *Common Sense* is an appeal not to the motley crew captured by the ordinary view but to the power of reason exercised by the understanding of each discriminating citizen-thinker about what is necessarily true.

The ordinary view in the eighteenth century is that the Lord appointed king and anointed aristocracy as proper rulers of the hoi polloi, who, after all, are just, well, smelly, ragged, dumb, and in need of direction from on high. Paine's genius: his argument that the common man is no commoner when it comes to individual rights and his grasp of necessary truth.

There is no fact, no information to enlighten Paine's (from *Common Sense*, the pamphlet that energized the Americans to revolution): *Society in every state is a blessing, but Government, even in its best state, is but a necessary evil.* This is no description, but advocacy of what is necessarily true, of good and evil, none of which is matter for eye and ear. This is analysis enforced by reason in appeal to the understanding.

There is nothing common here. It is all intelligibility, that sensibility for which there is no relevant empirical sense. This is not a matter of common sense, but of uncommon sensibility, that is, intelligibility. This is no matter of fact, but simply a matter of right and wrong.

Ambiguous, Ambivalent

1. *Ambiguous* and *ambivalent* seem similar but appearances are deceptive. The two AMBIs, like *ambidextrous*, seem in the common vernacular to ambulate interchangeably between one or the other. However, they mean oh-so-differently. *Ambiguous* is about the unclear meaning of words. That we are *ambivalent* is a metric that marks a uniqueness of the human condition.

Ambiguous means vagueness. Someone yells, *look out...duck!* Are they telling you to bend over, or are they warning you to beware a dangerous bird? Or, are they warning birds about hunters with guns?

Duck is ambiguous. Could mean a *bird*, could mean *bend over.* Ambiguity makes trouble by leeching clarity of meaning from our words, and so, from our thinking. Ambiguity is the enemy of cogency and coherence, of clarity and distinctness. Speak, think, indistinctly, ambiguously, and lose your world.

The oh-so-ordinary and conventional speech is fraught with, well, *it could mean this, but, on the other hand, it could mean that* - true in one case, false in the other.

Ambiguous, fuzzy, unclear speaking and thinking and we know not whether what we say expresses what we intend. The consequence is to keep us in the dark, separate from the world we intend to understand.

Reminds of George Berkeley's insight: *First we raise a cloud of dust, then complain we cannot see.*

2. We tempt *ambivalence* in the dilemma: if the one, then not the other. An easy example. Tonight, I will have pizza or lo mein. Like them both. Can't have both; must choose one or the other. Each is a clear choice—no *ambiguity* here.

Ambivalence over the road not taken: Is the road I took well chosen? We are the only self-made creatures. Only you and I become what we choose to be. All others, children and beasts, are innocent and do not know to deliberate over alternatives, and choose, perhaps against all instinct.

The purpose of an education: to learn our purpose, to learn what we need to know in order to choose well. Or, do not choose, remain innocent like the child and the beast.

But each choice invites a wake of regret for the path not taken. I know what you are thinking. Correct: You are not forced to choose. Innocence is not a choice but the absence of a choice.

3. Our world retires dark and hidden behind the blinding iron wall of *ambiguous* confusion. We can only know the world revealed by clear and distinct ideas as we learn from the Father of Modern Thought, Rene Descartes.

My favorite example of ambiguity is my favorite fallacy, amphiboly. My favorite amphiboly is by Groucho Marx in *Animal Crackers*: **One morning I shot an elephant in my pajamas. How he got in my pajamas I'll never know.**

Here's the vagueness that prevents clear and distinct meaning: Who is in pajamas? The elephant or Groucho?

Example II

The end of a thing is its perfection.

The end of life is death.

Therefore, death is the perfection of life.

See how it confuses, the *ambiguity* over the use of *end,* at first to mean purpose, a thing's virtue, it's what-it-was-meant-to-be, as in, *The end of a thing is its perfection.* And then, ambiguously, *end* is used to mean something quite different: the self-evident truth that all living things inevitably perish, as in, *The end of life is death.*

Example III

See how it confuses, the ambiguity over the use of *Nobody*. From Lewis Carroll's *Through the Looking Glass*: **Who did you pass on the road?** said the king to the messenger. **Nobody** said the messenger. **Quite right,** said the king; **this young lady saw him too. So of course, Nobody walks slower than you.**

In its first occurrence, *nobody* means *no one*, in the sense that no one is present. In its second occurrence, the same word *Nobody* now *ambiguously* refers to someone present by naming them. Their name is *Nobody*.

4. From the beginning of the West, and for more than two thousand years, our criterion for truth: Aristotle's *correspondence theory*. It seems so logically obvious: States of affairs take place in the world; Our own propositional assertion that so-and-so is such-and-such either does, or does not, correspond accurately, and is, hence, true or false.

But we are all Cartesian now, in the realization that our world can be gained only if our ideas of that world are unambiguous, clear and distinct.

Speak and think with words of alternate meanings and the world remains outside our reach, unknowable in *ambiguous* confusion. Make your words clear and your ideas distinct so that they are meaningful, a condition of possibility that they may be true.

Only in clear and distinct ideas can the truth of the world be revealed. So insists modern philosophy, which is certain that in ambiguous use of language we lose our world.

5. Consider this powerful, logical, deductive proof: If all S's are P's, and, if some individual x is an S, then, it must be the case that *that* individual has to be a P. Philosophers call this famous logical form of deductive reasoning a valid argument.

Grasp the force of this conclusion, validly proven. If an individual is an S, and if all S's are P's, then—of course!—that individual, which is an S, must also be a P. By its very structure the conclusion is inferred, enforced to be true if the evidence is true.

However, what makes the evidence true requires clear and distinct meanings for what is an S and what is a P—clearly and distinctly, and with no *ambiguity*.

6. Of clearly valid form, but ambivalent in meaning, is *American Indians are disappearing; This man is an American Indian. Therefore, this man is disappearing.*

By *structure* this is valid and has deductive force. But wait! That darn *ambiguity* loses our world. Notice: At first what is disappearing is the group of American Indians—at large. But the next use of *disappearing* refers differently—and *ambiguously*—to just one individual.

Of course, it is physically and logically possible to permit the truth that—at large—the group is disappearing, even though just one or a few have not yet vanished.

One test for the understanding of the above: There is no *ambivalence* in *ambiguity*; nothing *ambiguous* about *ambivalence*.

7. Ambivalence is the fork-in-the-road conundrum: Whichever path I choose denies the other.

Ambiguity: a vagueness that blurs and puts the world at distance from understanding.

Ambivalence: competing claims, perhaps equally compelling, gored on the horns of a dilemma; so human the quandary: which to choose, which to deny? *Ambiguity* is a whole other matter.

Language wants to make clear our way to constitute the (our) world but beware the obstacles of *ambiguity* and *ambivalence*. *Ambivalence*: Each *I-choose-this* necessarily requires that *I-deny-that* ... and perhaps all others.

However, there is reason to believe that we are never more human than when we choose between competing logical and moral claims. We are never more human than when we choose what is real and what is right, between the ugly and the beautiful, between what is noble and what is dishonorable.

8. No animal, only a person, can choose based on virtue and value. Do this and become the person you choose to be.

Philosophers from Kierkegaard and Nietzsche to Sartre and Camus argue that man is the only creature who can free himself from the crushing determination of un-thinking habitual behavior wrought by common sense and practical purpose. Only man, by his free will, is responsible to make himself to be, to become, what he has chosen to be.

What a becoming notion! Only man can, and to be a man, must choose to become a man.

Only we can decide against nature and nurture. Only we live deliberately and by our own decision. Only we be(come) what we ourselves decide to be. Only we are free to pursue this awesome and awful responsibility.

9. Awesome and awful? Heres' why. No elephant can fail at being an elephant. All that the elephant *is* is determined by its inherent physical structure and practical response to environmental circumstance. And yes, this sort of non-reflective life is very possible for you and me, and all too frequently is permitted by our fellows in a surrender to nature and nurture.

An awful responsibility! We are the only creatures meant to choose what to be(come).

10. Only we can choose, but ambivalence pervades the human condition. All other creatures are defined by nature and nurture and in no case are self-determining. But be prepared to pay the terrible price: Every choice denies its alternatives.

Choose pizza and deny lo mein. Choose a spouse and deny all others. Choose to live here and deny citizenship elsewhere. Choose allegiance to what you find most deserving and sacrifice others that want and need and deserve your devotion.

11. So important, this distinction between ambiguous, fuzzy, unclear speaking and thinking and the ambivalent competing claims to the true and the real.

If you do not choose you will not become a person. But every choice ambivalently refuses others, including others with rightful claim.

Ambivalent neglect of alternatives is the price we pay for exercising our humanity.

A life lived in quiet desperation says Henry David Thoreau. That is, lived not by choice, not by deliberate decision, but by mindless habit.

12. A haunting passage from a French existential perspective.

> **... [P]eople get married young. They go to work early and in ten years exhaust the experience of a lifetime. A thirty-year-old workman has already played all the cards in his hand. He awaits the end between his wife and children. His joys have been sudden and merciless, as has been his life...which is not to be built up, but to be burned up. Stopping to think and become better is out of the question.**
>
> Albert Camus, *"Summer in Algiers"* in *"Myth of Sisyphus and other Essays"*.

He no longer has choices to make. *They are off the table.* So is the terrible ambivalence so necessary to a soul-filled life.

The experience of a lifetime will soon be exhausted if experience of the world is limited to the everyday, mundane flood of appearance into eye and ear.

Played all the cards in his hand. No more to see or to say if seeing and saying is limited to and exhausted by ordinary business.

Easy. There is nothing easier than staying innocent and not bothering to build a life. Then, *stopping to think and become better is out of the question.*

A Note on Denoting

The trouble with *the*.

1. A little word, so useful to help us think and speak clearly. Logicians call **the** the definite article. ***The*** points to a possible subject for us to think and talk about.

Once something is identified as the subject we want to talk about, (*the King of France, the reader of this book*) then we can proceed to say something true or false. *The King of France is bald; The reader of this book will become smarter.*

Here is the traditional philosophical notion of truth: Predicate something true or false about the subject. Select a predicate that attributes to the subject some quality or characteristic, and, voila, truth. These subject/predicate assertions are true: *All men are mortal; The elephant is ponderous; A straight line is the shortest distance between two points.*

All*, *The*, *A: All very useful. There is no ambiguity in the use of the indefinite articles ***A*** and ***An***. But ambiguity infests the definite article ***The. The*** can indicate any one among a host of possibilities: *the reader of this book*. Or ***the*** can indicate just this unique individual and no other: *the King of France.*

2. Trouble begins when the definite article, **the**, is used to indicate only this individual and no other and is used to indicate that unique individual who happens *to not exist*. *Oi vey*, no matter what predicate is chosen, no truth can be said!

In *On Denoting* (1905), Bertrand Russell gave this example: *The present King of France is bald*. Of course, false. There is no such thing as the present King of France to be bald or hairy or anything else. So, it is false that the present King of France is bald.

More logical trouble in *On Denoting* (called the paradigm of English-speaking and English-thinking philosophical accomplishment): Logically, the denial of any falsity must be true. If it is false that *the cat is on the mat*, then, obviously, it must be true that *the cat is not on the mat*. But *the present King of France is not bald* is just as false as the assertion that he is bald!

Logic demands they cannot both be false! Not to worry. Russell unfolds a labyrinthine logical solution that saves language from the embarrassment false statements, the denial of which is also false. Let not the details of Russell's solution delay us.

3. More interesting, I think, are the views of definite descriptions by Russell's continental contemporaries, Alexius Meinong and Gottlob Frege. Nicely, it was Russell who brought both Meinong and Frege to international philosophical notice.

Meinong's view is that every definite description is meaningful and significant, whether or not it refers to things that do or do not exist. Language is a powerful thing. Let's notice that if you can name it, and it does not exist, that's a use of language that signifies ... what? ... nothing? Of course not! According to Meinong, even the *round square* is significant language that meaningfully indicates something, even if that something is an impossibility. To be sure, the round square cannot exist. But that is a limit of existence, perhaps of logic, but not of language, not of meaningfulness. Meaningfulness widens our world and extends beyond mere existence.

Yes, that something is round, and at the same time, square, is a contradiction. It cannot exist in the physical world. But, says Meinong, that's a limitation of the physical world; The conceptual power of the imagination has no such limit, and opens our understanding to so many more delicious possibilities.

4. I like to think of Meinong's *Theory of Objects* this way: Let's respect the power of language; You know what I *mean* when I say *round square*. That there cannot be such things places no limit on meaningful language.

Isn't Meinong correct in his view that it is true that unicorns have horns, whether or not they exist? Is it less true because they happen to not exist? Does the truth about things depend on whether or not a thing exists?

Meinong's analysis widens the realm of reality to include both existence and what he calls *subsistence*. A Meinongian non-existent entity *subsists*, and therein enjoys a sort of reality other than the reality of existing things. Does that make them *less* real? To subsist is to be meaningful, therefore, real, even though the subsisting thing does not exist.

Perhaps we need to rip them apart: existence and reality. Neither infers the other, despite our taken for granted assumptions about the world. Each reveal and intends something real about the world. If not the world, then perhaps our understanding hosts more than one sorts of reality: existent and subsistent.

It is correct that you cannot see subsistent things. Does that make them less than real? On what grounds? Perhaps it is a prejudice to think that just because you can see it, it is real.

5. More interesting, I think, more satisfying and more influential is Gottlob Frege's distinction between *sense* and *reference*.

Called *the most important paper in the history of the philosophy of language* (*You Tube,* Jeffrey Kaplan) Frege's distinction between *sense* (what a subject *means*) and *reference* (its *name*) is one of the most instructive insights into the nature of definite description.

Best to begin with this oft quoted example. In the evening, ships at sea steered by the always-north *evening star,* and in the morning by the always north *morning star.* Later it is discovered that these stars are the same heavenly body, the planet Venus.

The name *Venus* is a r*eference*, a name, a denotation. *Venus* refers to a thing by pointing to it. *The morning star* and *the evening star* do not denote, do not refer, but give the *sense* of thing. *Venus* is a *name. Morning star* and *evening star* give a *meaning: brightest star in the evening and morning.*

Test your understanding. *The morning star is Venus*: true. *The evening star* is *Venus*: true. *The morning star is the evening star*: false. What it *means* for something to be a daytime phenomenon, brightest star in the morning cannot also *mean* an evening event.

6. Meinong widens our notion of reality to include the plethora of real things that do not exist, but in their subsistence are no less real. This opens our understanding to the insight that meaning, not simply existence, is the measure of reality.

Then Frege brings us to see that it is simple and childishly easy to denote or to refer by naming things. But the more mature apprehension grasps what a thing means, its sense, and is measured by its essential nature.

7. The *sense* of things. Meinong and Frege make the sense of things clear so that we can ascend from the senses to sensibility. The common, ordinary view that limits reality to what exists, sadly, makes the world a small thing.

Atom

1. Is there an ultimate reality building block out of which all things are made? Behind the deceptive veil of how things look, behind the appearance of unending diversity is there one foundational principle shared by all things, unseen and unseeable, the ultimate building block of reality out of which all apparent diversity emerges?

This is the first question of science, first raised by the Greeks two and a half thousand years ago as they were about to initiate Western civilization.

Convinced that the appearance of things is deceptive, not real, and that reality is not to be simply described, but requires explanation, the ancient Greeks searched for the *archai* (are-kai), the fundamental organizing principles that render reality intelligible. Two and a half thousand years ago they analyzed, named, and proposed atomic theory as they initiated Western science and philosophy.

2. In 1908 Ernest Rutherford won the Nobel Prize in Chemistry for his experimental discovery of the atom, the astonishing insight that your fingernail and rocks and robins and air and water and all things, both alive and inert are made of atoms.

Shocking to common sense, all diverse physicality is made of the same stuff. At the minimalist level of quanta (the smallest possible bits of a thing) is a structural architecture of particles, which are identical to—

exactly the same!—as the particles that construct your fingernail and rocks and robins, air and water, and all things alive and inert.

3. Examine its smallest pieces (quanta) and discover that everything you think about physicality is incorrect. Ernest Rutherford to Niels Bohr, Nobel Prize in Physics 1922, discovered that the identically same building blocks at the minimalist level (electrons and protons and neutrons) but in different combinations of positively and negatively charged and neutral particles make up everything: fingernails, rocks, robins, air, water, and all things alive and inert.

We assume all that occupies our experience of the world is *real* as reported by the appearance of things. But the apparent diversity of reality is, well, a chimera. All physical reality is an electrically charged tension between swarming negatively charged electrons orbiting a positively charged nucleus, then rendered charge-neutral by a neutron glue holding the proton-nucleus together.

The scientific revolution, Rutherford to Bohr, proves that the minima—physical material's littlest bits, quanta—are identical for each physical thing, no matter how different they appear to our senses. The same omni-present particles, electrons, protons, and neutrons, but in divergent combination, construct all the things that occupy our experience of the world.

The so counter-intuitive truth: our sensible world is, we think, intelligible as it appears, but that is only for the practical purposes of common sense. The scientific truth: things are not as they appear. Their appearance is not even in them but in—and only in—our own experience of them. Reality does not exist, cannot be seen or heard by eye and ear, but can be apprehended by scientific revelation and intellection.

There is no red in the red chair, only a reflected wavelength of light which is not *red* entering our eye, traveling the optic nerve, and exciting the vision center of the brain to allow our experience of *red*.

Is it true that the red chair is red? Of course! But this is a truth about us, about our experience of the chair—not about the chair.

> *Those who are not shocked when they first come across quantum theory cannot possibly have understood it. Everything we call real is made of things that cannot be regarded as real.*
>
> Niels Bohr.

4. So shocking to common sense, which is always incorrect about such as *the true nature of reality*, it needs to be said again. All we see, hear, touch, taste, and smell, are *not* in the things we sense, not *in* the things themselves, but *in*, and *only in*, our own sensing of them! Our own experience of the world contains the world in that way experienced. Is there an objective world, separate and distinct, already constituted prior to our experience of it, waiting for us to know it? What evidence is there for that supposed objectivity?

Rutherford to Bohr revealed with empirical evidence and scientific investigation the true nature of physicality which has no resemblance to what we think is real. This shocking insight was first prophesized by the ancient Greeks more than two thousand years ago. Fifth Century B.C. Leucippus (Lew-sip-us] and his student Democritus (Dem-ock-ri-tus) had no science, no scientific method, no prior scientific achievement to aid the challenge they made to our so easy naïve realist surrender to the so vivid flow of factual circumstance that floods into and overwhelms eye and ear.

They only had their keen observation directed, protected, and promoted by their determination to disallow smug, easy, self-congratulatory superstition in attempting to know the world that they saw in all neighboring civilizations from Egypt to China.

Democritus realized that reality is not available at the fingertip of touch, color, and sound, but conjectured that, by this mental experiment, if only we could cut a thing down to its smallest possible bit and still retain its essential nature, then that cutting would give insight into what a thing really is (to cut, cutting: *tomas* in Greek—say toe-mahss).

Perhaps by examining the tiniest bit of it we may see behind the obfuscating appearance made by the mass of it. A cutting so fine that if cut again it would no longer be; *a-tomas* (cannot be cut again), the first hypothesized atom, possibly revealing the fundamental nature of reality, discovered and elucidated two and half thousand years later by Rutherford/Bohr, was first proposed by Democritus, the ancient Greek.

The theoretical atom, many with hooks so as to facilitate their various possible combinations which explain the otherwise random and mysterious assortment of diverse things that occupy our experience of the world, was first proposed by the ancient Greek, then discovered by modern science.

5. The ancient Greeks are patiently aware that the world to which we have direct and immediate access by eye and ear is a random swarm of circumstantial accident, like an unruly child, chaotic, full of flux and unpredictability.

The Greeks are the first to realize that sound knowledge of that apparent chaos will be gained only if we peel away confused and confusing appearance to make appear the *archai*, the first principles of logical order and regular form.

This first science and philosophy, invented by the Greeks, will evermore distinguish the East from the West.

This Western way of thinking is motivated by the realization that things cannot be as they appear since all we see and hear is random factual circumstance that could be other than it happens to be. The door is open, the apple is red, the cat is on the mat. Cat could be out hunting birds, the apple could be yellow, the door could be closed.

Indeed, *could be other than it happens to be* is a necessary truth about everything around us. This is what it means for a statement to be factual and is the definition of *information*. *Could be other than it is*, factual information that pervades all that we experience by eye and ear. Factual information contains no necessity and no essentialness. But both necessity and essentialness are necessary for the secure knowledge of things.

Yes, you can see things, and name them, and factual information is at your fingertip. A nice question: *Does that mean you know them?*

6. Here is the first necessary truth about things and the Greeks are the first to realize it. The Greeks are the first to realize that to know, to really know, to know what is real about things, is to know not just what happens to be the case but to know what is necessary about things.

For this earliest scientific attempt at knowledge-certain about our world, they proposed atomic theory. Twentieth century atomic theory proves them correct.

Things

1. *Why* are there things? *Why* do things exist? For good reason?

We are so certain that existence marks and measures reality. Existence and reality seem synonymous. *It exists, it's real; it's real, then it exists.* Science, technology, and most of all, common sense, are all certain that existence *is* reality, reality *is* existence. They mean the same! Science, technology, and common sense will not have it any other way. Without that undefended pre-condition (*reality is existence, existence is reality*) all three, science, technology, and common sense, cannot do their work and must give up.

Oh, the power of language. And when it goes awry, we can fall into confusion. A leading culprit: *existence*. Beware of this linguistic trickery. We think *it **is**!* And without thinking about it, the ***is**,* seems the same as *real.*

Let me say right away, plenty of things are real but do not exist: Zeus, the Headless Horseman, Pinocchio's nose. How do I know they are real? I can say true things about them! Is that not the test for reality?

2. *Why do things exist?* Do they have to? *Why Are There Things?* And how is it possible to know about them?

Albert Einstein reminds us:

The most incomprehensible thing about the world is that it is at all comprehensible.

It is logically and physically possible for nothing to exist. *Why* do they?

We are sure that things are prior to our encounter with them. In logical order: first the world, making it possible to see and know it. Our only direct and immediate access to things is through the physical senses. That leads us to think that if it is real, we can see, hear, touch and taste it. We think: W*hat* we see must first be there so that we *can* see it.

3. Reality is a happening place. Circumstance and happenstance flood into our senses. Therefore, reality must first happen, prior to our encounter with it, so as to be available for us to see it, hear it, touch it, describe how it looks, how it works—*know it.*

But ... w*ait!* ... an astonishing notion: What if it is the other way around? *What if what-is-real is not simply a matter of material presence to eye and ear. Perhaps reality is an essentialism, a matter of meaning that remains hidden behind appearance until revealed by the understanding.*

4. A double puzzle. There are things ... *why?* We know about things ... *how?*

A shocking notion: It could happen that no thing exists and nothing happens. This is not only logically but physically possible. There are real things which do not exist: triangles, Sherlock Holmes, his loyal friend, Dr. Watson, perhaps the Lord we meet in Genesis, perhaps Saint Paul who writes about Him in the gospels. Truths about all these persist independently of whether they possess and suffer physical existence. Correct?

I know what you are thinking. *If there were no existing detectives, we would have no pattern on which to model our understanding of Sherlock*

Holmes. I beg to differ. Your understanding of who and what is Sherlock Holmes does not require you to have met and experienced a living, existing detective. To understand who and what is Sherlock Holmes, it is required that you understand what it means *to detect.* The youngster reading his first detective story may well not have ever met a detective, but well understands the detective tale. Correct?

5. An astonishing notion: *What if our knowing about them—not just that they exist, but what they mean—is prior to, reveals what is essentially real, and makes possible that they occupy our understanding, and not just our visual experience?* And what if existence is not the mark of, but a blemish on and a hindrance to, a fully accomplished reality?

How becoming! I argue that things come to be, come to exist, so as to become becoming examples of their essential nature, and as well accomplished as the hardship of physical existence will allow. *Essential nature* is a meaning, and meanings do not exist, but, I believe, inspire things into existence. *Essential meaning*: the blueprint; physical existence, the emanation of the blueprinting plan.

I am not the first to say this. This is the Idealist Platonism and Aristotelian Realism that initiates the Western world two and a half thousand years ago.

6. As to the relationship between *we,* who are in the world, and the *world* we are in: The most common and casual view is that, first, there are things, then, second, we are abled, by a look and a feel, a hearing, a taste and a smell, to come to know them.

For now, let's pass by the troubling, but undeniable, scientific truth that what we see, hear, taste and smell is not in the things but in our own sensation and impression of things.

7. As certain as we may be perhaps this casual, common, taken-for-granted view is not only incorrect but exactly wrong. Perhaps things come to be, they be(come), they manifest *being* (in ancient Greek, *ontos*) in cooperation with the understanding that first intends, and then reveals their essential nature. Perhaps our knowing them brings them to the light of intelligibility, whether or not they exist.

8. This so anti-intuitive view is hinted at by the most powerful, and most romantic, argument for God's existence. St Augustine's (early fifth century) ontological analysis argues we need only *think* correctly about God, about *what He means*, and His reality is proven.

The definition of what the Lord portrayed in Genesis means, omniscient and omnipotent: that being of such perfection that none greater can be conceived. So, if He does not exist, He could be greater still. Therefore, not only is it true that God exists, but—by the logic of His very *being*, His *ontos*—what God *means* proves, and ineluctably, that He *must* be.

The famous *Ontological Argument* to establish that God exists hints at the notion that meaning is the foundation, the origin and explanation, the inspiration for existence.

9. Perhaps we need to distinguish *being*, reality from *existence*.

For Christians: the omniscient (all-knowing) and omnipotent (all powerful) Lord of Genesis thinks so fully, so completely, a thing's definition that how could it not burst into physical existence, exemplifying God's idea. How could the full and complete definition contemplated in the all-knowing mind of an all-powerful God not inspire a physical world populated with existing examples of that essential meaning?

The same argument for secularists, with Divinity, making full and perfect expression of their best possibility, fulfilling the role of the

Christian God, inspiring all physicality to come to be and achieve the promise of that definition.

10. In his autobiography, the twentieth century's most famous philosopher says that in his youth, he found the Ontological Argument convincing. So do I. Dear reader, do you? Later, Bertrand Russell, so thoroughly committed to *existence* as the true measure of *reality*, gave up his earlier admiration for the notion of perfect *ontos* (the meaning of being) inferring God's existence.

Here's what I think. *It doesn't!* When the Ontological Argument is understood to explains reality, proving that the Divine, how Good is something, requires that something to be, that is, to be real, it is undeniable.

I agree that the notion of God's existence is, well, problematic.

11. I do not think that existence and reality are the same, and admire investigations into non-existing realities. I believe the *Ontological Argument*—proving that reality emanates, emerges, is explained by its origin in and creation by divine being—is undeniably valid. It is, of course, logically and physically possible for there to be nothing—no existing things. I know, a strange notion, but why does it seem unlikely? Why is it likely that there be things? Is it a requirement? If so, for what reason do things come to exist, occupy our experience of the world, and bring us to ask about their origin?

An invitation to an answer by St. John, **In the beginning ...**

... The saint does not say that first God separated the land from the waters, and then populated both with creatures ...

John says, **In the beginning was the word ...**

*... the **logos**, ancient Greek for reality-revealed-by language ...*

... and the logos was with God, and the saint ends with the rapture:

And the logos was God.

Oh! Again! **And the logos was God.**

12. Begin by seeing things as metaphor for knowing them. There is reason to believe that we are mistaken in our casual view that the object-seen is separable from the act of seeing. You have no evidence that the apple seen to be red continues to be red when not seen. Only this is certain about the redness of the red apple: Its redness is in, and only in, your seeing and not *in* the apple aside from and outside your vision.

What is *in* the apple that causes you to see that it is red? Redness? Of course not. Basic science assures us that in (better, *on* its surface) the apple is a reflected wavelength of light (*which is not red*) that causes us to see its redness. Its redness is in you, not in the apple. *How* you see participates in *what* you see.

How you know participates in—determines—*what* you know.

Reality known is a moment not separable from the act of knowing. Seeing and knowing participate in that which is seen and known, by forming and shaping visual and intellectual apprehension.

The thing-seen and the seeing of it, the reality-known, and the uniquely human grasp of reality are moments of each other, and require each other.

13. All sentience is capable of simple awareness. Thinking outside of language is a poor thing.

> *Language is the medium in which we are conscious. The speechless beasts are aware, but they are not conscious. To be conscious is to "know with" something, and a language of some sort is the devise with which we know.*
>
> Mitchell, Richard, *Less than Words Can Say*.

Only through language can we distinguish the necessary from happenstance, the excellent from the ordinary, and that which is more achieved and accomplished. Although language delineates and permits incisive analysis, linguistic habits of expression can deform and delimit the scope of thought.

We say and think that if *it is* then *it exists*, falling to the equation that *is* and *exists* are equivalent. Better to say and think: *It is real. It is real* more open-mindedly invites the possibility that reality contains not only existing things, but also, real things that do not exist.

The gnarly tree exists, but its gnarliness does not. Is its gnarliness not real? If its gnarliness does not mark and measure the tree's reality, what does? The empiricist answer: the number of its leaves, branches, and roots. Does anyone interested in the tree's reality want to make a count of all the leaves it has lost during its long-lived physical existence? Could anyone, would anyone, make a count of leaves, or branches, or roots, over the century of its existence, and claim that now—aha!—we know it better?

14. Most moderns agree that *existence is not a predicate*. To say *x exists* in no way amplifies the understanding of what x is.

Gilbert Ryle's delicious philosophical insight: Saying *Satan does not exist* is not about Satan in the same way that saying *I am sleepy* is about me. If there is no Satan, then the grammatical subject of that claim has no referent.

Ryle argues that since there is no Satan, there is no thing that this sentence is about. Ryle's conclusion: Every sentence of the form *x exists—x does not exist* exemplifies *systematically misleading expression*. To avoid systematically misleading expressions, beware of predicating existence, or non-existence, to anything. Existence is not a quality of a thing, like its color or shape. To speak as though existence is a quality, like color or shape, is to make, systematically, a Ryle-ian misleading expression.

Ryle's example, *Carnivorous cows do not exist,* is about ... what? Carnivorous cows? But of course not! It cannot be about carnivorous cows - because there are none! How can a statement be about something that, well, *isn't?* Avoid this systematically misleading form of expression; do not say, or think, that *Carnivorous cows do not exist.* When tempted to this category error, make way to clear thinking: *Cows are not carnivorous.*

15. The understanding wants to know *what* it is, *what* is its nature? *What* is it for? *What* would it say if it could reflect and talk? Let us note that answers to these questions reveal a thing's reality, whether or not the thing happens to exist. Perhaps existence is overrated. Perhaps existence is but happenstance and accidental to that thing's essential nature.

16. Sisyphus does not exist, nor do the gods who condemned him to the hell of the human condition. But absent his heroic Olympic tale, we cannot well know what it means to be a person.

Is Existence Overrated?

Part I. Is reality presented to the senses, or grasped and intended by the understanding?

1. We are so certain that if it is real, it exists; and if it exists, it is real. What is not real does not exist; and yes, what does not exist cannot be real.

Existence, reality: a distinction without difference? No. They are not equivalent. Not hardly. Reality does not exist, and I argue, a thing's existence does not bring its reality. Reality is a meaning—a thing's reality is its meaning—and meanings do not exist.

Things exist and make an appearance of color and sound, etc. to eye and ear, etc. Do meanings appear? Can a meaning be, say, red, or loud? Can a meaning be located in space and time as must every existing thing?

The apple exists and we think its redness is a mark of its reality. Does redness exist? The apple is apparently, in some sense, out-there. Is its redness out there? Or is its color in us, in our own impression, determined by the way our vision works? On the surface of the apple is a reflected wavelength of light (which is not red) but of just the right size (wave length) as to cause us to see red—so says basic undeniable science.

Existence brings reality? But existence is manifested by, and only by, sights and sounds, feels, tastes and smells, none of which are in the things we see and hear and smell and taste but in, and only in, our own seeing, hearing, tasting, and smelling.

So vivid and insistent is the appearance of things that their physical characteristics overwhelm our helplessly receptive senses. So vivid, persistent, and intrusive to eye and ear, we think that existence is the mark and measure of reality.

2. But why do things exist? Do they have to? *Why are there things?* And why is it possible to know about them?

> **The most incomprehensible thing about the world is that it is at all comprehensible.**
>
> Albert Einstein.

It is possible for nothing, *no thing*, to exist. Why do they?

We think that logically things must come first, must arrive to our experience fully constituted, full of existence, fully real so that then we can come to know them. Seems obvious. Things are prior to and present themselves to our encounter with them, and thereby make possible, our knowledge of them.

Things are real because they occur. No one asks: *Why do they occur?* Reality is a happening place. Circumstance and happenstance flood into our senses. We see, hear, touch, describe how it looks, how it works, and believe this is how we come to know it.

But ... wait! An astounding and unnerving notion, what if it is the other way around? What if *what-is-real*, and the reason for its reality, remains hidden behind the deceptive veil of appearance[1] until revealed by the way we experience it? Let me explain and elaborate on this astonishing notion.

3. A shocking notion: It could be that nothing—no things—exist. That is not only logically but physically possible. There are real things that do not exist: triangles, Sherlock Holmes, perhaps the Lord we meet in Genesis, perhaps Saint Paul who writes about Him in the gospels.

All these are real. How do I know? I know truths about them, and I am persuaded by the notion that if you know truths about x, then x is, must be, real, whether or not it exists. Truths about all these persist independent of whether they possess, or suffer, physical existence. Correct?

The Austrian philosopher, Alexius Meinong, suggests we should enlarge our notion of reality to include not only things that exist but, as well, real things that do not exist. Let's say they *subsist*.

4. An astonishing notion: What if our knowing them—knowing *what they mean* - is prior to and informs how they occupy our experience of them. What if their best possibility inspires them to be and informs how they came to exist? We will remember that non-existing mastodons and existing elephants, and whether they exist or not, in no way informs us about or adds to our understanding of those ponderous beasts.

5. I said *informs*. Not a casual notion. For physically present existing things, as well as non-existing subsisting things like triangles, Sherlock Holmes, and Saint Paul, to know them—to really know their essential nature—little help comes from the appearance they would make if they existed...correct?

After all, as basic science assures us, how they (happen to) appear depends as much on how works our eye and ear as depends upon them. To *know* means to apprehend a thing's best possibility, it's very meaning, which does not exist, and is not advertised in the tumult of the constantly changing physical world.

What makes a thing to be real? What informs our knowledge of things...what we see or what we understand? Does seeing help us understand? Or is existence a blemish, as existing things are, like pebbles in a stone polisher, alas, thrown all about helter-skelter?

6. Philosophers call this view *idealism*, first fully articulated by Plato in Athens, fifth and fourth centuries BC. Western civilization begins in this first fully articulated philosophical analysis of both the world and who and what we are as knowers of the world.

7. How becoming! I argue that things come to be, they come to exist as examples of their essential nature. How do I know? Just watch them! Each existing thing, especially sentient creatures, are constantly striving to become as well-accomplished as the hardship of physical existence will allow. Is this too romantic a notion?

8. Essential *nature* is a meaning and meanings do not exist. Meanings reside in the realm of the divine, or, if you like, in the omniscient mind of an omnipotent God inspiring physical things into existence.

Things come to be because they are meant to, whether by God's Grace, or (for secularists) by divine and ideal essential meaning. Essential meaning is the blueprint, the plan; physical existence is the emanation of the blueprinting plan, so full and complete in its definition of things that they cannot help but be(come).

Divinity—what Plato called the realm of the Good and Christians call God in His Heavens—is home to perfectly formed definitions fully articulating the essential meanings of things (what Plato called the *Forms*). How then, can individual existing examples resist bursting into existence exemplifying those perfections?

I ask again, what makes a thing that occupies our experience of the world to be real? Is it the vivid and insistent physical intrusion of their appearance into our helplessly receptive sensibility? Or is it by way of coy and patient understanding, seeking to be educated, and informed about essentialness? Isn't it through the understanding that we intend the essentialness of things hidden behind the deceptive veil of appearance revealed if and only if our educated understanding intends it?

9. Essential meaning, the blueprint, the plan; physical existence, the emanation of the blueprinting plan, so full and complete in its definition of things that they cannot help but be(come).

How real is an existing thing? Plato: *How good a one is it?* When we say, *Wow! That one is a beauty!* We are talking about how well it represents its essential meaning, about how real it is ... correct?

I ask again, what makes a thing that occupies our experience of the world real? Is it the vivid and insistent physical intrusion of its appearance into our helplessly receptive sensibility, or is it by way of coy and patient understanding, seeking to be educated, and informed about essentialness? Isn't it through the understanding that we intend that essentialness of things hidden behind the deceptive veil of appearance and revealed if and only if our educated understanding intends it?

10. As to the relationship between *we*-in-the-world and the *world*-we-are-in, the most common and casual view that we are so certain of is that, first, there are (must be) things in the full regalia of color and sound and existential appearance, and then, second, we think it undeniable, that is how and why we are abled, by a look and a feel, a hearing, a taste and a smell, to come to know them.

We think that knowledge is a fabric of familiarity.

For now, let's pass by the troubling but indubitable scientific truth that what we see, hear, taste and smell is not, appearances to the contrary, in the things but in our own sensation and impression of things. A moment's reflection on basic, undeniable science and we realize that, of course, the red of the red chair is not in the chair. On the red chair is a reflected wavelength of light that causes us to see red.

11. As certain as we are, the common view is not only incorrect but exactly wrong. Things come to be, they become, they manifest being (wait for it…) in cooperation with the understanding that first comprehends and then intends their essential nature, the source of and inspiration for them to be(come).

Oh, that's too heavy, and very compact, and so anti-intuitive, and should be read again…slowly.

Our knowing them brings them to light—to the light of *intelligibility*. What a becoming notion! What a responsibility! Dear reader: too romantic?

Perhaps knowing a thing is an act of love, of revelation. If we do not know them, then their reality remains dormant. Perhaps knowing them, in any fullness and intimacy, requires that we intend (that is, grasp by the understanding) their essential nature which cannot be seen but only understood.

Part II. Begin again.

12. Existence. *Reality.* The same? What a terrible, but so pervasive, mistake. We are so certain that reality exists and that if it does not exist, it cannot be real.

Let's pause at the obvious. If it exists, it makes an appearance that floods the senses. By eye and ear and with odor, touch, and taste—these impressions, these disparate pieces of sense data are our only direct and immediate access to the objective world; to the world we are so certain is out-there, fully constituted, prior to, separate and distinct from and ready for encounter by our subjective access to it. *It exists, it appears, it is real,* and that access is primarily by eye and ear, and with feel, taste, and odor.

On the other hand, and on the contrary, *reality* is a more amorphous notion. When we say that something is real, we are not talking about anything that we can see; it is difficult to say how and why it is real. Easy is the leap, *it is* to *it is real.*

Existence, you cannot miss. *Reality,* you cannot find it unless you look for it.

Reality is a meaning, and meanings do not exist. What exists has a shape to feel, a color to see, a sound to hear. What color is *real?* What does *real* look like or sound like?

Existence makes a physical presence for eye and ear. *Reality,* like all meaning, requires a pro-active exercise of the understanding. *Existence is* right there in front of you. *Reality*: if you do not look for it, you will not find it.

13. My argument (I think it obvious, and not in need of defense) is that existence is obdurately present for all of us, for children and for beast alike. On the other hand, your search for reality by understanding opens you to become a person and renders the world not only physically present but intelligible.

I deplore our traditional, easy, obsessive, and intuitive commitment to existence-as-the-metric-of-the-real while disregarding the difficult but so much more revealing doctrine that what makes a thing real is not that it exists (see the essay just prior, *Is Existence a Proper Predicate?*) but rather how well it accomplishes what it means to be one of its kind.

14. This most romantic, and if you are devoted to the view that existence is the epitome of reality, most compelling argument for God's existence: The Ontological Argument. I admire most Descartes'

version: *God, by definition, means the most perfect being; if He did not exist, He would not be perfect; therefore, God exists.*

How elegant! In this invitation to an adventure in logic, we need only to think correctly about God, about what *He means*, and *His existence* is proven.

Dear reader, I know you will understand that I would prefer, *His perfection guarantees His reality.* That is, God means *the most perfect being; if He was not real, He would not be perfect. Therefore, God is real.* Uh ... wait ... make that *divine goodness* is the source for and explanatory foundation of reality.

Again, The Ontological Argument is the most elegant and romantic and persuasive argument for why it is necessary for divinity to be real since its first formulation by Saint Augustine fifteen hundred years ago.

Things exist; God is not a thing. I think that the notion that God exists should offend the Father of Modern Philosophy (Rene Descartes) with his rationalist suspicion of unreliable existential appearance.

15. There's a certain romantic and elegant logic to this ontological argument. From the Greek, *ontos*, (the unseeable but knowable nature of a physical thing) the *meaning* of a thing's *being*, the *meaning* of its *reality*, shifts focus from *existence* to *essential meaning*. The perennial question of Western organized religion *Does God exist?* is pursued by the more pressing pre-question: What do you *mean* by *God?*

I like the logic of it. If we are to talk about God, we need to know what it is we are talking about! I like the method of the ontological argument: *What does God mean?*

It is argued that what God *means*...the Lord portrayed in Genesis...omniscient and omnipotent ... the most divine and most real being of such perfection that none is greater... that then He must exist! Here's why. *If He does not exist, then He could be greater still.* Therefore, not only is it true that God exists, but—by the logic of the *meaning* of His very being, His *ontos* (to say it in the language of Plato)—what God *means* proves, ineluctably, that He must be.

He must be? The Ontological Argument, ever since Augustine, concludes, *He must exist.* I prefer, *He (divinity) must be real.*

The famous ontological argument to prove that God exists hints at the notion that meaning is the foundation, and inspiration for existence. Oh, my! Make that *reality*, not existence, and I am persuaded. The Ontological Argument cannot be denied.

That is, not only is divinity real, but it must be real, as the origin and source for all that exists... for the very possibility of existence. Divinity renders existence intelligible.

16. We need to distinguish between being (reality, *ontos* in the ancient Greek) and existence.

My position: The ontological argument to prove God's existence is deliciously elegant in its methodology of meaningfulness and is logically impeccable but works to prove the unacceptable view that the Lord of Genesis suffers existential blemish, as do all things that suffer the rigors and hardships of physicality.

God—a physical existence? The notion violates my sense of reality. I have no doubt about the reality of divinity, needed by intelligibility to explain physical existence. Does God *exist?* I will leave that question to others, even while I admire the attempt made by The Ontological Argument to prove that He does.

Convinced I am that divinity is not only real, but necessary. How else to explain that there are things?

I believe that divinity (call it God if you like) as the source and explanation for why there are things is better thinking. For you Christians, perhaps the omniscient (all-knowing) and omnipotent (all powerful) Lord of Genesis just *thinks* a thing's full and complete definition. He envisions it so fully, so completely, how could it not burst into physical existence with individual examples of that complete and perfect definition. How could the full and complete definition not welcome a physical world with physical examples of that essential meaning?

So charming. By this so romantic view, existence is purposed as matter of exemplification.

For you secularists, the same argument, but with Divinity, pure Goodness (perfect expression of essential meaning) fulfilling the role of the Christian God, inspiring all physicality to come to be and achieve the promise of their essential meaning. By this so romantic view, goodness (*how good a one is it?*) marks and measures existence.

17. It is, of course, logically and physically possible for there to be nothing. I know, it's a strange notion, but why is it likely that there be things? Is it a requirement (if so, from where and for what?) that things come to exist, occupy our experience of the world, and bring us to ask about their origin?

An invitation to an answer by Saint John, *In the beginning*...

Notice, the Saint does not say:

First God separated the land from the waters, then populated both with creatures...

John says:

In the beginning was the word, the logos (ancient Greek for reality-revealed-by language)...

*... and the logos was **with** God,*

And the logos was God.

That is, *In the beginning* (refers to the origin of all things) is the *intelligibility* of God's word. His recognition of the goodness of things makes them to be.

18. How does reality *begin*? How do things become what they are?

Is it a requirement that there be things? If so, from where and for what? A fair comment: it is altogether remarkable that things come to exist, occupy our experience of the world, and bring us to ask about their origin. It is a fair question: how and why do things begin? How and why do things be[come] what they are?

19. Begin with seeing things as metaphor for knowing them. There is reason to believe that we are mistaken in our casual view that the *object seen* can be torn away from the act of seeing. Someone says, *I am seeing. Seeing what? Nothing, but I am seeing.* Well, and obviously, that is not possible. If you are seeing, there must be *something-seen*... correct?

Similarly, *reality-known* is a moment not separable from the act of knowing and can be separated only conceptually. *To know* is to know something, just as *to see* is to see something.

Seeing and knowing participate in and are necessary ingredients to that which is seen and that which is known. What is seen and what is known cannot be torn away from the act of seeing and the act of knowing. Tear away the thing seen and the thing known from the act of seeing and knowing, and then there is nothing you can say about such things now independent from our encounter with them. This philosophical view, the doctrine of *intentionality*, is argued by the school of *phenomenology*.

20. All sentience is capable of simple awareness. Only with language can we distinguish the necessary from happenstance, the excellent from the ordinary, the more achieved and accomplished. All these are central to what it means for something to be real. All these require language. Although language delineates and allows incisive analysis, linguistic habits of expression can deform and delimit the scope of thought.

We say, *it is, it exists,* and we fall to the equation that *is* and *exists* are equivalent. Better to say and think: *It is real. It is real* more open-mindedly invites the possibility that reality contains not only existing things, but, as well, real things that do not exist.

The gnarly tree exists, but its gnarliness does not; is the gnarliness not real? If its gnarliness does not mark and measure the tree's reality, what does? The empiricist answer: the number of its leaves, branches, and roots. Does anyone interested in the tree's reality want to make count of its lost leaves in all its long-lived physical existence? Could anyone, would anyone, make a count of how many leaves, or branches, or roots, over the century of its existence, and claim that now—aha!—we better know it?

21. Most moderns since Descartes agree that existence is not a predicate. To say *x exists* in no way amplifies the understanding of what *x* is. *X is, it exists* says nothing about *what* x is—only *that* it is ... correct?

The understanding wants to know *what* it is. What is its nature? What is it for? If it could talk, what would it say? What would make it to be a better one? Let us note that answers to these questions are equally, if not more, revealing of a thing's reality, whether or not they happen to exist. Perhaps existence is overrated. Perhaps existence is an accidental happenstance to that thing's essential nature. Perhaps the empiricist's favorite metric of reality, is non-revealing of what a thing—really!—is.

22. Sisyphus does not exist, nor do the gods that condemned him to the hell of the human condition. But absent his Olympic tale of heroism,

we cannot well know what it means to be a person. He does not exist, but by knowing him, we better know ourselves. Is he not, then, real?

* * *

[1] The first to say it this way: Galileo.

Is Existence a Proper Predicate?

What sort of truth is it to say that something does—or does not—exist?

Mastodons used to exist—no more. Does the truth that they used to exist... *exist?* When they existed, did the truth that they exist also exist? *What is truth? Where is truth?* I like best: *How are truths true?* Things exist, and like mastodons, sometimes go out of existence. When they go extinct does the truth about them go extinct?

> *If a person thinks or asserts something true, what is there about what he thinks or says that makes it true? What, in short, is truth? These questions can seem unspeakably deep; they can also seem unspeakably trivial. That is one good sign that they are philosophical. Another is that they are puzzling.*
>
> George Pitcher, *Truth.*

Ask, *Where is truth?* and be led to the new question, *What is truth?* This way of thinking makes us realize that truth is not a thing. *Things* are *out-there*, the truth about them is not. *Where is truth?* Out-there? Clearly not. Things are *out-there*; truth is not a thing and not *out-there*. In us? No, it is still true even when I am not thinking about it.

Perhaps truth is a *relationship* between we who know the world and the world that we know; between what is in us, in our understanding of the world, and the world about which we know truths.

1. Yes, yes, both science and common sense must assume (whether correctly or not) a steadfast and objectively real *out-there*, but philosophically, *where is that? How do you know that?* With philosophical caution and a healthy skepticism that demands a defense for one's beliefs, I can confirm the contents of my own impressions and ideas, but that they are caused by things *out-there* requires demonstration and defense. I don't have one, do you?

What do we know for certain? Perhaps there is an *out-there* containing things, but if so, the truth about them is not there. Things exist; the truth about them does not. That things exist, or not, is informative about their physical state, and their availability to eye and ear, but perhaps this is just a factoid, and does (or does not) inform us about what it means for a thing to be one of its kind. If he existed, would Sherlock Holmes be a better detective?

2. Elephants are ponderous, live in matriarchically ruled herds, and are thought to possess fabulous memories. Elephants exist. All true. And all these statements—each in the same grammatical and logical structure—appear to be all true in the same way. Each picks a subject, *elephants*; each goes on to predicate—say something about that subject—*are ponderous, live in matriarchically led herds, have fabulous memory,* and *exist.*

It seems that each informs us about elephants. It is true and informative that *elephants are ponderous*. It seems to us just as true and informative, and in the same way true and informative, *elephants exist*. And so, we think, *ponderousness* and *existence* are equally determinative of what it means to be an elephant.

Predicate (say pred-eh-*kit*), as a noun, names the property of things. *Predicate* (say pred-eh-*kate*), as a verb, is the meaningful linguistic act of attributing that property to a subject. Predicate (pred-eh-*kate*) accurately and, voila, truth.

Elephants are ponderous, elephants exist, both true, but equally determinative of what it means to be an elephant?

Each statement above talks about elephants—the subject. Each then attributes (*predicates*) to elephants a description or quality or insight about the subject, elephant. A properly used predicate will indeed *inform* about the subject. For example: *Grass is green, snow is cold, rocks are hard.*

3. This is an important distinction. Some truths, like the truths above, are descriptive of how things happen to look. Contingent truths report happenstance, the appearance physical things make to eye and ear. Contingent truth report what could be other than they [happen] to be. Happenstance is *contingent truth.*

Contingency and happenstance are a weak sort of truth, unrevealing of a thing's essentialness. It is true that some apples are red, but they do not have to be, as green apples are eager to point out.

As you read this, please, dear reader, bring this insight with you: *x exists* is a contingent truth, a piece of happenstance. Let's note that *x exists* says nothing necessarily true about *x*.

Are there truths about the things that occupy our experience of the world that are both *necessary* and informative? I think that, even if true, that a thing does, or does not, exist, is not informative, and then, of course, not necessary.

It is true that mastodons no longer exist. But does knowing that bring knowledge about mastodons similar to your knowing something significant about elephants? It is a fact that mastodons do not, and elephants do exist. But this is a trivial truth, a factoid, and brings no essential knowledge of those ponderous beasts.

I like the above use of *in-form*: *to infuse with meaning what is necessarily true of a thing*. This is opposed to what we tend to think is knowledge: lots of contingent, factual information, facts that report happenstance and accident as though the red of the red apple reveals anything about its apple-ness. Green apples agree.

It is true that mastodons no longer exist, but elephants do. Does that inform about mastodons and elephants?

4. But ... wait ... elephants are large, mostly grey, with long snout; all this is informative about their physical appearance. That they make loving caretakers of their children and live contently in a hierarchical social order ruled by their matriarch, informs us about their nature.

Which brings us to know, to really know, to know what's real? That oh-so-easy and unavoidable appearance, all of which is contingent, happenstance and could be other than it happens to be, or grasping their essential nature, their what-it-means-to-be one of their kind? Contingent appearance or what is essential and necessarily true. Which gives us reality: familiarity or understanding?

Elephants exist. True? Of course! Does this truth bring us to better understand elephant-ness?

We know that mastodons do not exist. Does that fact tell us anything about mastodons? What does it mean to be *informed*, to know about something? Is information, perhaps lots of it, enough to claim knowledge of a thing? To know what an elephant is, do you have to know something necessary about what it means to be an elephant? Or is it enough to know lots of facts: big and heavy, mostly grey, long-snouted, etc.?

Do you know yourself?

5. To this I hope we will all agree. There are things, and they have properties. Things exist; their properties do not. The red chair exists; its redness does not. Being red correctly predicates a quality of the chair and is true—not about the chair—but about how we see it.

Do facts, information, and lots of it—lots of contingent truth—including the fact that something does (or does not) exist, bring us to know?

Let's touch on the important note that *the chair is red* is true, but not about the chair. Rather, it is true about us, about our experience of the chair. That is, it is true that we see it to be—better, *to appear*—red, but that redness is, according to basic undeniable science, in our seeing. The red is not in the chair, but in us. In (better, *on*) the surface of the chair is a reflected wavelength of light (which is not red!) but of just the correct wave length to make the optic nerve, and vision center of the brain bring us to see the chair as red.

6. The redness of the chair is a truth about us—about our experience—and not about the chair, in its separate-from-us objective reality. This leaves the grueling question: If the red is not in the chair, but in us, together with all its other physical properties we gather by sight and sound and touch, etc., then *what is in the chair?* Is there anything inherently within and intrinsic to the chair's objective reality?

What is in the chair—separate and distinct from how we [happen] to see it? What marks it to be a chair and measures how real a chair it is? How about *how good a chair it is?* Surely the mark and measure of reality is something other than, something more than, *it exists*.

Does the red chair possess any quality or property or attribute that is not only true but *necessarily* true of what it means to be a chair? Such reflection raises the suspicion that existence is not a proper predicate, at best, a factoid and not revealing of what is necessarily true of things.

7. I think, I hope, we will agree. Properties of things—the red of the red chair, the ponderousness of the elephant—are to be contrasted with individuals that possess them. To predicate is to attribute a property to a thing that has them. If the predication is accurate, then the resulting statement—*elephants are grey* and *that chair is red*—is true. True but, in these contingent cases, trivial.

More trivial: *elephants exist.* You and I are the only creatures gifted with the capacity to know essential, necessary truth. I think you will agree: *What a responsibility!*

8. Is existence a property that individual subjects either have or do not have? What do you say about *carnivorous cows do not exist?* Is existence a property that our subject fails to have? But that cannot be, according to the early twentieth century English philosopher, Gilbert Ryle. According to Ryle, this impossibility is not just because there are no carnivorous cows, but because there cannot be such things. *Carnivorous cows* are no proper subject; there cannot be any such thing. Therefore, you cannot say anything meaningful about them, including trying to say that they do, or do not, exist.

Better to say *There are no carnivorous cows.* It is a confusion: C*arnivorous cows do not exist.* More correctly, it is not possible for them to exist, because there cannot be any such thing. The very idea of carnivorous cows is a self-contradiction. Their essential nature, cows are herbivores, therefore, how can things that could not possibly exist possess any property?

A proper predicate must inform about its subject; if the subject is inconceivable, no predicate can be proper for it. We see, again, meaningfulness rules intelligibility.

Let us note: *carnivorous cows* are inconceivable, unintelligible. Nothing meaningful can be said about them, let alone that they do or do not exist. A nice little logical lesson: intelligibility is paramount in our capacity to know.

To know—to know really—to know the reality of anything, happenstance, appearance and what happens to be the case: none of this will do. To know—to really know—to know what is real requires that we know what is necessarily true of a thing.

Carnivorous cows are no things and cannot be the subject of any attempt at truth.

But ... wait ... listen to what I just said: Yes, *things exist*, but ... hold on ... their predicate does not! And their existence, or non-existence, is irrelevant to and utterly non-informative about what they are, about what they are ... really!

Is Seeing Believing?

Part I

1. Arithmetic is about numbers and astronomy is about stars, what, then, is philosophy about? *The things that occupy our experience of the world* has defined the primary subject matter of philosophy as philosophy was turned modern by Rene Descartes in the mid-1600's.

We tend to think that *things* are prior to, objectively and fully constituted previous to, and unaffected by our ideas of them. Descartes makes philosophy modern with his oh-so-simple yet obvious-once-you-say-it grand insight: Our only access to *things* outside us is through our own ideas inside us.

The Cartesian revolution makes us modern, and prepares for the grand contemporary philosophical insight: You can be certain about the content of your own ideas and impressions. You can be certain about your own subjective life. There is no doubt that you have this or that idea. But there is much doubt as to where that idea comes from; skepticism, the hallmark of modernity.

In its multi-millennial tradition, philosophy had given priority to things. The traditional first major branch of philosophy, metaphysical ontology (from then Greek *ontos*): the nature of the being of things. *The reality of things*, the traditional priority of philosophy. But ... wait ...

our only access to things is by way of our own ideas, and modernity begins.

The first major concern is (was) about things and their nature. Things first, and the correct understanding of their *ontos* leads to and determines the nature of the knowledge of those things. First metaphysics, then, logically, epistemology, the investigation into the nature of knowledge.

Along comes the Cartesian Subjective Turn in the mid-seventeenth century and philosophy will never be the same.

In both his major works (*Discourse on Method*, and *Meditations*), Descartes takes pains to make us aware of the obvious unreliability of impressions. His so convincing example: *From a distance the square tower appears round*. Truth-certain is the goal of modernity, and my impressions, gained by the senses, could well be just imaginings and no more certain than my other attitudes and beliefs.

Enter the famous dark possibility of the malevolent but powerful demon who could fool me into thinking I am awake while actually I may logically, and possibly, be dreaming that these hands with which I think I do my work are real.

The truth is that physicality is an appearance, and all appearances are suspiciously subjective. Yes, the rock appears solid, the snow cold, the grass green; are my impressions of these hard, cold or green? By what warrant am I certain they are caused by a prior and dependably objective world *out-there*?

Now that the moderns—yes, all moderns—realize that ideas are not just a representation of something (some thing) out-there, but a subjective mental event and our personal possession, we also realize that by no warrant are ideas tied to and responsible to well represent a prior objective truth out-there. The new philosophy, birthed by Descartes' *Subjective Turn*, must pursue modernity's first question: *Which of our ideas are true? Are any of them certainly true? If not, then what to do?*

2. Modern philosophy realizes that to know about the world one must begin with our access to the world. So, now: *What makes our ideas of things reliable?* Descartes' revolution of modernity leads, in a hundred and fifty years, to the contemporary concern: *Does the nature of seeing and understanding determine the world in that way seen and understood? Does our experience of the world shape the world experienced that way?*

Or, as the conventional view would have it, *does the world-experienced remain outside of our experience of it, obdurately and objectively unaffected by how we experience it?*

3. Ever since it matured to modernity, philosophy focuses on our ideas and impressions of those things, again, as they occupy our experience of them. Are our impressions and ideas *caused* by things that are—really!—*out-there*? Later philosophy will ask: *How do you know there is an out-there, out-side of our experience* filled with objectively enduring physical things? We are heading to the question: *Which of our ideas are true? What kind of a truth is it if based on nothing more than the appearance things make to eye and ear? Does* seeing *justify* believing?

Do you think (and I think you do) that our impressions and ideas are true because you assume they come from and are caused by a dependably objective physically real realm outside your experience of the world?

4. Is there an *out-there* out there? I know you think so. As for me, I am not sure. Have you evidence for your belief? Or do you so believe because it makes the experience of things easy? Are there things *out-there*

that cause our experience of them? How do you know that? You know which ideas you have; how do you know where they come from?

We will all agree: things seem to be out-there. Where is *out-there*? I see, hear, feel, touch, taste and smell things that seem to me to be out there; Do I similarly sense the *out-there*? Has it a color to see, a sound to hear, a taste or a smell? Everything (every thing) has a color; what color is *out-there*? Is there an *out-there* out there just because, well, there must be an objective counter point to and cause of what is inside you?

Part II

5. Philosophy knows, we will all agree, that whether or not things are out there, our experience of them is bifurcated into two radically diverse ways through which we encounter them. On the one hand we receive the appearance they make to eye and ear, and on the other hand, by the pro-actively revved engine of the understanding, we apprehend their essential nature, their what-it-means-to-be-one-of-their kind.

The latter description of the work of understanding is dense and should be read again. The claim I make is that understanding does not simply encounter but engenders and reveals the reality of what the senses encounter. Vision receives what we take to be the appearance of things; the understanding looks behind appearance, lifts up and away that deceptive veil (appearance) and engenders explanation for things.

6. It is important to note that these two boulevards of access to the world have nothing whatsoever to do with one another. Seeing and understanding are as different as awareness and consciousness.

Curiously, we prize the former over the latter. Why curiously? Example: that the red apple is red has utterly nothing to do with what it means to be an apple. I know, a strange phrase, *what-it-means-to-be-an-apple*. But what makes the red apple to be—really!—an apple? That it is red? But ... please ... wait ... there are equally real green apples.

I insist: What makes it to be—really!—an apple. Appleness! Which, of course, you cannot see. I insist: the test of how real an apple it is has nothing to do with how it looks but is measured by its inherent and intrinsic character: how-*good*-an-apple it is.

I know what you are thinking. *Can you say what is appleness?* The answer is *no*. Nor can you say what is love and what is lust, but you know them when you see them. And I know that I bring to my seeing what is needed to know the things seen. Proof? My dog, Doogie, sees as well as I but he does know what these things are.

You and I know what is a table and what is a chair and we know what these things are for. But Doogie cares not a whit if I sit on the table and write on the chair.

7. Philosophy's traditional first question: What marks and measures a physical thing to be real? The appearance (I know—so vivid and vivacious!) that floods into eye and ear, or a thing's essential nature as apprehended by the understanding? Are things inspired into existence by the full and complete definition (Plato's ideal *Form*) that indicates how good a one they can be? Or are things Aristotelian explicable and understandable as the consequence of causes, Formal and Material, Efficient and Final? That is, do we know things by knowing who made them and why, and for what purpose?

8. I think we will agree that all truth received by eye and ear is circumstantial, happenstance, contingent; it could be other than it appears, than it happens to be. Truths intended by understanding, which truth is hidden under the deceptive veil of appearance, reveal what is necessary about experienced things, either idealistically, á la Plato or by Aristotle's realism.

For your consideration: Empirical sensation (seeing and hearing, touching tasting and smelling) brings, not knowledge, but, at best, familiarity.

9. I say to my student who confesses to adopting the perverse and pervasive belief that seeing is believing: What is real about you? All that we see in a snapshot is irrelevant to the essence of you. We see only that you are tall or short, blond or brunette. Do we see that you are a fine representative example of what it means to be a person, a woman, a mother ... we do not. Do we see your essential reality? Can you *see* what it means to be a person? You cannot.

As a woman, femininity is your essential nature; it defines what you are but does not appear in any physical, factual description. More significantly, it is not just happenstance, it says what is necessarily true.

Your femininity is what is necessarily true of you. How you happen to look, how you appear to eye and ear are contingencies that make no contribution to who and what you are ... are really.

Believing is easy; seeing is easier. Seeing is helplessly receptive of random information. What you believe ought to be based on more than what you see.

Sense and Sensibility

1. The *senses*, shared by all creatures, man and beast alike, provide immediate and direct access to the world. *Sensibility*, unique to man, apprehends what is essential to things rendering them intelligible. The *senses* see; *sensibility* understands. The helpless *senses* receive information that describes happenstance, what happens to be the case. The pro-active *sensibility* renders our world intelligible.

Sense and *sensibility*, they sound similar, as though one grows from the other, but nothing could be further from the truth. The *senses* see, touch, hear, smell and taste; sensibility, *intelligibility*, apprehends what is essential and necessarily true. Sensibility engenders and intends what cannot be seen: the inherent and intrinsic essential truth of things.

The senses feed our awareness with facts, descriptions of how things look and how they work. The senses make us aware of happenstance, of circumstance, but we cannot see essentialness, what is necessarily true of things.

2. My sort of philosophy thinks nothing is more significant about a thing than what is necessarily true, how-*good*-a-one-it-is. Its value, how *good*, how *beautiful*, how *well achieved* it is requires the intentional power of the understanding which is responsible for rendering things intelligible.

I can see (as can all creatures with the correct cones in their eyes) that this particular apple happens to be red. *Happens* to be. Some are green. That this one happens to be red is, well, information, but is in no way essential to what it means to be an apple. No one can see what it means to be an apple, but with the power of understanding you and I can *know* what it means. *What it means to be one of its kind* is not information, but necessary truth, not to be seen but to be understood.

3. Consider what the senses receive and then consider what the understanding renders intelligible. The intent and accomplishment of the understanding to apprehend the essential truth of things has no similarity whatsoever to what the senses receive from the appearance of things.

Don't overlook the different vector (going *to* it or coming *from* it): what we see and hear is *from the world to us*; what we understand is generated by the engine of the understanding and is *from us to the world*. Sensibility intends the world's *meaning*. Nothing is more real or more true about things than *meaningfulness*.

Helplessly, but easily and with no effort, the senses receive data in the form of brute fact. Facts, information, physical description of how things look and how they work is not revelatory of the essentialness that renders a thing meaningful.

We *see* color and shape and movement; we do not see what a thing means. We *understand* what a thing means and what it means has utterly nothing to do with how it appears to the senses. What a thing means does not appear alongside its size, shape, or spatial and temporal location.

Subjectively within us are the physical senses; they gather sense data, including sights and sounds, into our awareness which we then mistake to be objective substantialities and objectively true of the things we see and hear, smell, taste, and touch. But the sound of the tree falling to generate a clap of thunder is not *out-there*.

The sound happens in us, within our senses, *our* perception; sound is a mental event. Basic science assures us that there is no sound out there,; out there is only a vibration of air.

Does the falling tree make a sound? Of course! Sound is a subjective presence within sentient awareness. If no one is within earshot, there is no sound, but the vibration of air remains objectively present, whether or not anyone hears it.

4. We mistake what is by sense and subjectively *in us* (such as colors, tastes, sounds) to be the sensible, intelligible objective reality which is *outside* us. The terrible error of common sense: it is certain that our subjective sense of things is caused by, and is a reliable report of the objective world outside us.

How our seeing and hearing work is responsible for what we see and hear. Not the things seen and heard, but *how* we see and hear, is responsible for *what* we see and hear. Example: whales and dolphins lack the appropriate cones in their eyes and do not—cannot—see color.

Does the red apple have anything to do with your seeing that it is red? Of course! But on the apple there is no red, but a wavelength of reflected light (which is not red) that causes the correct electrical impulse (which is not red) to travel the optic nerve to the vision center of the brain, and, then, finally, red!

Our biggest blunder is the certainty with which we are sure that what we see and hear is mark and measure of an objective truth *out-there*. That is the view of my sort of philosophy; that is the view that defines *rationalism*. The opposing view, pervasive throughout the English-speaking world ever since the eighteenth-century English Enlightenment, that the truth of things is reported by the sense, is called *empiricism*.

5. *Out-there?* Where is that? To be sure, we can be certain of the content of our own impressions and ideas, but by what warrant can we defend the notion that what we see and hear is mark and measure of an objective reality *out-there*, outside of seeing and hearing?

Rationalism wonders: Why do we fail to weigh the low significance of matters of fact received by the senses, compared to the deep significance of the intelligibility and necessary truth of things that cannot be seen? Why do we make so terrible an error?

Terrible? Because only the understanding—not the senses—has access to reality itself. The senses can only point to things, name them and describe how they look; each necessary to the work and goal and purpose of common sense. Their essentialness, all necessary truth, requires reason and understanding, and cannot be seen, and is but an obstacle to pursuing the ever-present common sense task at hand.

Because only within this mistaken view (there is a world out there occupied by things, the reality of which—we think—is given by sight and sound) can common sense direct its work of problem solving in our day-in and day-out living. Common sense thinks there is an objective world out-there; why do you think so?

The point is, we are desperately in need of a philosophical analysis of existence. What's real? What exists? Clearly, reality and existence are not synonymous. Do we really access the reality of things, as empiricists insist, through sight and sound or, as rationalists argue, only by rendering their reality through the understanding?

6. Two-and-a-half thousand years ago hints are made of the terrible significance of the need to separate sense from sensibility by the most savory thinker before Socrates, the aphoristic Heraclitus.

Harken not to me, but to my logos [language!] ... **listen to the logos** [the divine reason that orders the cosmos and gives it form and understandability] **and make the meaning of the most common, yours.**

That is, be not overwhelmed by empirical experience, no matter how vivid and vivacious, no matter how irresistible it might seem.

Much information does not teach wisdom.

That is, facts, even those verified by witness to be true, do not gain, earn, or deserve to be deemed the essential reality of the things seen.

The ears and eyes are poor witnesses to men if they have barbarian souls.

We must not act and speak like men asleep.

That is, nothing by eye and ear can gain entrance into the understanding. Perhaps all by eye and ear has no more substance than a dream.

Everything happens in accordance with the logos. It is hidden until the thinker reveals it. The hidden harmony is better than the visible.

Heraclius hints at the coming Greek invention of Western science and philosophy. That is, intelligibility, which cannot arrive visually, but only in the vehicle of language, overwhelms fact and description if the goal is the essence of things and not simply how they happen to appear.

7. The world is a happening place, overcrowded with existing things, and all of it is not only unavoidably present, but is about to overwhelm our senses. We are certain that nothing is so true of a thing as the contingent fact that it exists. But ... wait ... what does it *mean* that it exists? What but that we can see them, hear them, and taste, touch and smell them? Are you certain that makes them to be real?

Speaking above is my favorite philosopher, George Berkeley, as pure an empiricist as you can want. Berkeley partners with his epistemological rival Rene Descartes to install *The Subjective Turn*, the foundation upon which all modern thought begins. (Berkeley is a leading light of English-speaking empiricism; Descartes fathers modernity with his rationalism.)

Berkeley's subjectivism is so extreme, that is, so pure, he is justly said to be an *idealist*. That is, he believes it indubitable that only ideas of things are real. The things they are ideas of are real? A Berkeley-ian would ask: *How do you know that?*

8. The philosophic tradition, before Descartes and Berkeley, is decidedly and unabashedly metaphysical, focusing on the foundational explanation of the reality of things. From whatever quarter, philosophy turned itself on with the first philosophic question, the metaphysical query: *What makes a thing to be real?* Reality itself invites philosophic speculation.

Descartes and Berkeley, the fathers of modern philosophy and thought, ignite philosophy's proper beginning. Yes, the philosophical concern is reality itself, but as Descartes writes to a friend: *My only access to things outside me is by the ideas in me.* That is, logically, subjectivity precedes and make possible our access to objective reality. Descartes devises our modern notion of *idea* as a mental event, a personal possession fathering both philosophical modernity and modern psychology.

9. If you can see it, it exists; if it exists, you can see (touch, hear, taste, smell) it. And seeing, touching, hearing, tasting, smelling are, of course, subjective manifestations of what we are so certain is the objective truth of things outside us that, we are sure, are the objective, substantial source of our ideas.

In the objectivity of their factual existence they obtrude, insistently, persistently, and rudely, if you will, upon our five physical senses. To be sure, our perception of them defines what it *means* that they exist! But ... wait ... does our perception grasp what they *are*?

What to make of the fact that the apple is red, the thunder is loud, and the water is tepid? Red, loud, tepid: marks of reality? Or are they manifestations of a seeming contact with the out-there? After all, perhaps God manages our ideas and impressions and arranges them into the interconnected chain of causality that we are sure to notice.

Berkeley (the Bishop of Cloyne) thinks so, and says that there is a God-arranged pre-established harmony between our ideas and the God-like staging of an *out-there*.

10. Your common sense says there are objective things existing *out-there*, causing our impressions and ideas of them. What possible evidence have you for this very comforting but indefensible idea? Just where is *out-*there? How does their existence *cause* anything?

Why are we so certain? How do we get fly-trapped into such outlandish ideas of the primacy and priority of an external world that dictates and determines our experience of it? It works like this. We notice things, then we ask about them. We ask the wrong question.

Berkeley advises the modern thinker: Do not ask (of the things that occupy our experience) What *are* they? Rather, ask: What do they *mean*? With this insight, Berkeley joins and advances the Cartesian invention of modern thought.

11. Let's revisit the question: Why are we so devoted to existence as the bellwether of reality?

[i] Our only immediate and direct and unavoidable encounter with things is by eye and ear. We take for granted that what we see (and

hear and touch, etc.) is determined by the things seen and heard and touched, but there is no evidence for this! There is irrefutable basic scientific evidence that what we see and hear is more determined—ultimately determined—not by the things themselves, but by the ways in which our own seeing and hearing work.

It is time to shift our attitude toward our experience of the world with a heightened emphasis on how we understand the essential nature of things, rather than how they happen to look.

[ii] We hold common sense in such high esteem, and it can do its work only under this pernicious prejudice of a pre-supposition that things are—really!—real as they appear and, *out-there*, and really out-there, really real just as they appear.

[iii] Is there really an *out-there* out there? Did your common sense make that up? Is there any evidence on which to base an *out-there* other than that common sense needs it?

Read on, dear reader. Read on.

Cause

In 1964, Supreme Court Justice Potter Stewart said he could not say what obscenity is, but *I know it when I see it.* What is causality? I cannot say. Can you? Do you know it when you see it? What does it look like?

1. Nothing so reveals the tenure and timbre of a philosophical view as how it thinks of causality. Every proposed understanding of causality is shaped and driven by the flavor and perspective of the philosophical view that forms it and every philosophical view is pointed in its direction by its view of causality. Each seduces the other.

Example: Empiricists believe that things are as they appear. Things that occupy our experience of the world have color, shape, make a sound, have an odor that allows us to experience them. Obviously, causality is no such thing. Causality makes no appearance to eye or ear.

All things are of some color; What color is *cause*? How does it smell? *Okay. I get it. Cause is not a thing.* Wait! If reality is given to us in our direct and immediate access to the world by eye and ear, and if cause cannot be seen or heard, then is it irreal?

The seventeenth century empiricist English Enlightenment held that cause is *not* real, and *not* needed to be real for a fuller understanding of our world and how it works. I don't believe that. Do you?

2. The leading lights of classical British empiricism, John Locke, George Berkeley, and most of all, David Hume, are, must be, skeptical as to the proposed reality of *cause*.

Empiricists believe we know a thing is real because we can see it, hear it, touch it, taste it, smell it. That is, the empiricist believes that reality is revealed in our empirical encounter with things. All will agree that cause is no such a thing, but rather a connection between things.

What sort of thing is *connection*? An eager empiricist insight: If things are real, and reality is given to us by the appearance things make to eye and ear, then the connection between them, like *cause*, is not a thing, and, therefore, not real.

3. Aha! By its very meaning, what sort of connection is *cause*? A *necessary* one! Ever since Aristotle, that has been the definition of cause; what cause *means*. But, as advocated by the English Enlightenment, Locke to Hume, necessity plays no role in reality. Hume's famous question: *When we say that one event causes another, do we have anything more than a regular sequence of events?* One after the other, the other preceding the one, and no exception to that regular order of events. Then we read necessary connection into that sequencing events.

That is Hume's unassailable modern empiricist argument against the traditionally accepted conventional Aristotelian view. You call it *cause*, one bringing about and responsible for the other, but all you can see, witness, and confirm is the regular sequence of events. By what evidence does your intuition show them to be causally connected?

Cause, as a necessary connection between things, is not itself a thing, nor a necessary connection between things, but a phantasmagoria of your intuitive imagination that seeks explanation about things.

One cannot deny that Hume is on to something here. You cannot see *cause*. But continental rationalists protest. Descartes to Spinoza to von Leibniz defend the rationalist insistence: What marks something to be real is what is necessarily, not accidentally, true of it. What makes something to be real is not how it happens to appear, but how well it achieved is its inherent, intrinsic and necessary essential nature.

4. Event A: *I let go.* Event B: *It falls.* The conventional view: We believe my letting go (and, of course, gravity) *caused* it to fall. Again, cause is not a thing but, we are certain, a connection between things. Hume's empiricism (things *are* as they *appear*) disagrees. Hume's famous pool table example: On the table are cue ball, eight ball and events, the cue ball striking the eight ball just right, and the eight-ball falling into the corner pocket.

The pool table and player and pool balls are *real*. Is there a real *cause* somewhere on the pool table? The eight ball is black, the one ball is yellow. Does cause have any characteristic or attribute, sensible or otherwise, by which to know it? Or is *cause* a phony notion made-up by your intuitive need to make the world sensible?

5. On the other hand, take the romantic rationalist view that things are real, not by their physical appearance and descriptive circumstance, but by their inherent intelligibility. Then, of course, causality is not only real, but a requirement of the intelligible structure of the world.

Real is the cue ball and *real* is the eight ball, but *really* real, meta-real, is the causal connection that illustrates and illuminates intelligibility. The cunning pool player and his fine stroke with his pool stick *caused* the eight ball to fall into the corner pocket.

Degrade the meaning of cause, says the rationalist, to be merely the witnessable report of a sequence of events, with no inherent connection between them, render the world unintelligible, a random series of unconnected circumstantial events.

6. Let's begin again. Is causality a useful notion?

The notion of causality is useful to make sense of things, *and* useful to understand this or that philosophic perspective. Want to find out about a philosophy? No better entrée to its thinking than its understanding of causality.

Let's note that Newton's Universal Law of Gravity describes what happens, i.e., physical bodies attract each other as a function of their distance and mass, but does not, cannot, say why physical bodies are seduced by each other, nor can it say what is that perplexing causal connection.

Oh! the limits of science. Another reason to go to philosophy when you are driven to know the way and the why of things.

7. Four peaks of philosophical achievement. Plato's romantic *idealism*; Aristotle's down-to-earth, scientifically inviting, *analysis-of-the-world-on-its-own-terms, realism*; the oh-so-*skeptical* English Enlightenment; Immanuel Kant's *transcendentalist* formation of contemporary thought.

Each brings a very different understanding of causality. Each is terribly persuasive and provocative as they promote, and are promoted by, their so different world views. Each a bellwether ringing a truth of their epochal time, from the ancient to the contemporary world view.

Part I: Idealism

8. Plato lays the foundation that initiates Western civilization. Nothing is more real than the *Good*. Together with the full definition of things, the *Good* inspires, *causes* all things to be; causes all existing things to become the hope and promise of their definition, of their *Form*.

The reality of things flows from a *formal* plan that inspires them into existence. Their existence instantiates that inspiring plan. The blueprinted definition of their virtue inspires them to be(come). They are real because they well represent what they mean. The Good sees they are god-like; the gods see they are good. That's how and why they come to be.

The question for romantic idealist Platonists is not *what is real* or *what is irreal*, but, for each existing thing, *how* real is it? How *good* a one is it? How beautiful?

That is, in Plato's weltanschauung, the Good and the True Definition of things (their *Form*) are primary and prior substantialities responsible for reality to be(come).

How becoming a notion! Reality is a *becoming*, inspired, and caused by the full, formal definition that cannot be complete until realized by individual existing instantiations.

9. The word for *cause* in ancient Greek is *aitia* which refers to the who or the what that takes responsibility for whatever consequential result is thereby explained. The keyword here is *responsible*. To the Platonic understanding, to cause is not just to bring about a consequent event. That's just too physicalistic a view for the romantic idealist. To cause is to inspire a thing to take responsibility for how good a one of its kind it will *be(come)*.

Yes, the world of our experience is a happening place. But Newton's description would not satisfy the Platonic yearn for explanation of *why* things happen. That they happen as a gravitational function of distance and mass leaves the romantic Platonist, well, cold.

Romantic Platonic idealists are committed to the view that cause is not just an agency that makes effects arrive, but an act of love, like a blueprint is responsible for the building constructed to meet its hopes and desires. The Forms define so thoroughly the essential meaning of things that they cannot help but burst into existence.

10. The Platonic notion of causality is adopted in whole and wholeheartily by Christianity. Plato's Good becomes Christianity's God. Plato's Formal Definition, demanding to be completed in the world of existence, resides in the all-knowing mind of an all-powerful God. He need only think what things mean—omnisciently, all-knowingly, and omnipotently, all-powerfully, then in a loving appreciation, how could things not burst into existence?

The Platonic notion of cause, imbued with the ancient Greek sense that causes are responsible for their consequence, renders so easily the Christian notion that the Lord makes to be what is Good and True.

For Plato, nothing is more real and efficacious than *The Good*, which is other-worldly, pure and perfect, universal and eternal, previous and prior to the mundane things it *inspires* into existence.

Plato is no empiricist; His idealism relies on divinity as cause of, and inspiration for physical reality. Four hundred years after Plato, Christianity says that we and our world need to be responsive to the word of the Lord.

The Good causes things to *become* by making them responsible to well-represet their definition, their very meaning.

11. This idealist sense of cause thinks that the very nature of being (*ontos* in Greek) contains within it a hint as to its origin, an idealist ontological argument. Things are in the business of striving to be as good as they can be given the hardships of physical existence.

Part II: Realism

12. Aristotle's notion of causality both develops and redirects Plato's *Good* as the inherent *worthiness* of things in a very non-idealist, empiricist insistence on explaining things in their own terms. Down-to-earth is Aristotle's four-part doctrine of causality.

Plato's key concept, *The Good,* is appropriated, extended, and repurposed by Aristotle as the *worthiness* of a thing, its virtue. Aristotle estimates how well a thing achieves its purpose, its *telos,* its end, its *raison d'etre.*

For Plato, the idealist, each thing is measured by how good-a-one it is. Aristotle, the teleologist, knows what things are by understanding their end, their purpose.

For Platonists, the Good informs, sources, inspires, causes the very being of things. Teleologist Aristotle has a more realist view: *It is required that we examine things in their own terms.*

Both Plato and Aristotle measure the reality of things by their meaning. Plato's meaning is an agency from on high, from the divine—Christians will call it heaven—realm of perfect definition where *The Good* rules. Aristotle works in the world we know by and through our living in it, judging things by how well they achieve their purpose, by their virtue, their *arete* of accomplishing their end, their purpose, their *telos.*

13. Aristotle's notion of causality comes closest to our contemporary realist way of thinking. For Aristotle, as for us, causality is the very mortar that holds together the building of reality. For Aristotle, as for us, to know a thing is know the interconnected plethora of causes that explain not only its origin but what and why and how it *is.*

Central to his world view is his doctrine of the four causes: the *formal* and the *final,* the *material* and the *efficient.*

These two doctrinal couplets are needed to explain the very being of a thing. The *formal* cause is Plato's idea (ideal) of it, held, not in Plato's heavenly realm, but in the mind of the sculptor who does the chiseling, aiming the production to its purpose, its *final* cause.

The *formal*-and-*final* cause, but, too, the *material*-and-*efficient* cause, the mortar cementing reality into a skyscraper.

Obviously, a statue is made of some kind of stuff, perhaps wood, or stone, or something else. Whatever stuff is chosen is its *material* cause. And who chose it? Probably the sculptor, the maker of the statue, its *efficient* cause.

Part III: Skepticism

14. Consequentialist by theme (*causes have effects!*) the Aristotelian is closest to our contemporary view of causality. Most alien and anti-intuitive to our current way of thinking—but I think, by a logic undeniable—is the argument about causality made by the lights of the skeptical English Enlightenment. The key word here is *skeptical*.

The tenure of the classical eighteenth century, hard-nosed (and I think hard-hearted) English-speaking analytic revolution: Before you leap to your beliefs, be careful that what you say is meaningful, clear and distinct, not only intelligible but defensible. What does it *mean* that event A caused event B? From the English-speaking empiricist world view: *What does that cause look like?*

The bellwether of modernism: *be sure that what you assert is meaningful—or withdraw! What does it mean to say that event A caused event B?* Does that mean anything other than, as a sequence of witnessable events, A always preceded B, and throughout our experience, B happened after A? To this empirical view—things *are* as they appear—it must seem that the notion of *cause,* if in any sense intelligible, is a matter of happenstance, and of no necessity.

My view: Necessary connection is what it *means* to say that A caused B.

Empiricists say the notion that cause is a necessary connection between A and B is a leap of our intuition trying to explain our experience of the world. *Cause* is a phony notion made-up by your intuitional need to make the world acceptably intelligible.

But no one who claims to have experienced the causal connection between consequential events can say what it looks like other than there is, in our experience, a constant sequence of witnessed events. The speaker is David Hume, the most prestigious and oft quoted Irish empiricist of the English Enlightenment. Dear reader: is what Hume says undeniable?

Part IV: Transcendentalism

15. Nose itches, I scratch. What possible connection between mind and matter? The great puzzle: How is it possible that the itch *causes* the scratch?

The magical, mystical, inexplicable connection between mind and matter has haunted philosophy since its beginning. Descartes too. He says that reality is bifurcated between two mutually exclusive substances: mind *that thinks* and matter *that is extended. Mind* and *matter,* the two substantialities; mind, un-extended and matter that does not think. We are a mind that thinks, and, too, a body that is extended. Everything and anything true, significant, or meaningful about the one is utterly irrelevant to the other. Of course, they are connected. I itch, I scratch... How is that causal connection possible? No sensible answer from Descartes or anyone else.

16. Hume's oh-so-persuasive, and perhaps undeniable analysis that no warrant can be established for a necessary causal connection between consequential events *awoke me,* says Kant, *from my dogmatic slumbers.*

Neither Kant, nor anyone else, has shown Hume to be incorrect! Causality has no physical characteristic as do things detected by eye and ear. Within the empiricist view of reality, *causality* names, well, nothing, *no thing.* Rationalism insists that cause must be, otherwise we lose the intelligibility of the world. *Cause*: real or not? Can the necessary causal connection between antecedent and consequent be not be real?

But, of course, it *is.* Now, *how* is it? Now, Kant!

17. For almost two centuries before Kant, the philosophical battlefield mounted a raging war between the mostly British classical empiricists (*reality is present to the senses by its appearance*) and the mostly French and German romantic rationalists (*reality is necessarily known by the innate power of the understanding*).

18. What is transcendent in Kant's Transcendental Idealism? The seemingly impossible divide between the objective world and the our utterly dissimilar subjective experience of it. How to transcend that incompatibility? Kant points to the enormous achievement of Copernicus, and offers his own *Copernican Revolution.*

> *... [I]t has been assumed that all our cognition must conform to the objects; but all attempts to find out something about them a priori through concepts that would extend our cognition have, on this presupposition, come to nothing. Hence let us once try whether we do not get farther with the problems of metaphysics by assuming that the objects must conform to our cognition ...*
>
> Critique of Pure Reason.

That is, as Copernicus so successfully asked that we consider the Sun, not the Earth, as the fulcrum on which to understand the physical heavens, so let us focus on *cognition* of reality as the fulcrum upon which to understand reality.

Each, the sensibility and the understanding, make justified claim to touch reality. Each is vital, necessary for explanation of human knowledge. Neither knows how to acknowledge the other. Why? *We've been asking the wrong question!*

The question is not, *How do we know the world?* The question is, *What makes reality knowable to us?*

Kant's grand insight of contemporary philosophy deserves another read.

> ... [I]t has been assumed that all our cognition must conform to the objects; but all attempts to find out something about them a priori through concepts that would extend our cognition have, on this presupposition, come to nothing. Hence let us once try whether we do not get farther with the problems of metaphysics by assuming that the objects must conform to our cognition ...
>
> Critique of Pure Reason.

What an insight! We can only know about things what is knowable about them! What is knowable about them is determined, not by them, but by the understanding! Whew!

19. Review. First the Cartesian modernist emphasis on the priority of the *idea* of things, over the things. That prepares for the startling Kantian insight that our ideas *contribute to* and help *constitute* the intelligibility of the things that occupy our experience.

How? By demanding that things seen and heard by eye and ear conform to the demands made by the structures of sensibility and understanding.

First, modernity, ushered in by Descartes' *Subjective Turn*. First the modern focus on our own idea as entrée to what is necessary and true (*My only access to what is outside me is through the ideas in me*).

Is knowledge of things made by awareness of their physicality, or understanding of their essentialness? This is the century and a half-long unresolved debate between empiricist and rationalist.

Then Kant: *What is it about things that makes them knowable?*

Here's Kantianism. Here's contemporary philosophy: *What is it about cognition, about how we know, about the nature of the understanding, that makes objects-seen, and objects-known be seen and known?*

Here's Kantianism, here's contemporary philosophy: We do not just encounter our world, *we constitute it!*

20. Transcendental? *Transcend* the chasm of apparent disconnect between the objective and the subjective. *Ascend* to the realization that the objective world we know does not stand in opposition to, but invites and requires the pro-active intention of our own subjective knowing of that objective reality.

Kant and causality: Cause is not a thing; It is not out there, nor is it, so to speak, *in us*. What I just said is true, but a mistaken preconception lurks in and mis-flavors what I just said. To ask of causality *Where is it?* is to misunderstand the issue. Things can be located; Cause, the necessary connection between events, is not a thing and cannot be located.

Causality is, well, a *meaning*. A meaning that the structure of the understanding insists things must meet, must conform to, as though they are —really!—in necessary causal connection ... that is, if we are to know them. What things? Well, of course, things that occupy our experience of the world.

Cause, a foil we wrap around the world of our experience. Causality is a bridge-of-understanding that allows us to walk over the seeming chasm separating objectivity from our subjective knowledge of it by rendering it intelligible.

Could there be a causal connection out there cementing the necessary connection between cause and consequence? Could be! But that speculation is noumenal asking about things-in-themselves, outside our ken and outside the possibility of knowing about them. Let the reason dwell on such speculation, but the understanding can deal with, and only with, phenomena, with things that, first, we see and hear.

21. Conclusion. It is tempting to try to decide for one or another theory of causality. Dear reader, I suggest: *Do not!* None can be shown to be true, and the others false. Each is a profound revelation of the philosophical development up to its time. Each deserves to be relished for its sheer persuasive elegance. Know about these high historical moments and know about our civilization. Let each of these theories of causality firm and confirm the grand philosophical insight: *How we know the world determines the world in that way known.*

As you would try on a new jacket or skirt, let your understanding try on one or another explanation of causality and discover a different world. The world you know is the world you intend; intend it to be structured —or skeptically unstructured—by this-or-that notion of causality and meet a new world.

Out There, Part One

Is there an *out-there* out there?

1. The trouble is language that leads, structures and shapes and makes possible our thinking. Nouns name things. So, we tend to think if we know the name of a thing there must be a thing so named. It is correct that nouns are an important part of language, that, indeed, name things. It is not correct that all things so named exist. Logically speaking, grammatically speaking, *Carnivorous cow* is a perfectly proper noun naming not only what does not exist, but what cannot possibly be.

Carnivorous cows are not out there. You also have no cogent evidence to support the view that there is an *out-there* out there.

Out-there is a noun; but the *out-there* is not a thing. Things are located in space and time; they possess shape, color, texture, etc. You can see them. What does the *out-there* look like? Can you describe the *out-there* the way you can describe things you take to be out there?

Perhaps there are things out there, but, dear reader, if I give you that (for your intuitive comfort) please consider that the *out-there* is no such a thing, and cannot be cogently understood to be out there the way mountains, monkeys, mice and men are out there.

2. I hope you noticed that if you give up the view that there is an *out-there* out there, then there is nowhere to place mountains, mice,

monkeys and men outside of your ideas and notions of such things. Yes, we know truths about these things; perhaps those truths are limited to our own ideas of these things.

I am not the first to say this.

3. Does what is *in-us* demand that it be a consequence of what is *outside us*? One leading light of the eighteenth-century English Enlightenment, and co-founder of modernism in philosophy, the Irishman, George Berkeley says: **No!** *You think so,* says Berkeley, *because you do not think aright about existence. You think of existence as a brute fact, a noun which names a thing. But you can be certain only of your own perceptions of things, and you have no warrant to posit there be really real objective things out-there causing those perceptions.*

Berkeley's view astonishes—and perhaps even upsets and insults—common sense. But I think a fair-minded assessment will agree: Berkeley's argument for his radical idealism is undeniable. Love, dear reader, to hear what you think.

4. What is philosophy about? As astronomy is about stars, arithmetic is about numbers and biology is about life, traditional philosophy is about, well, things. What things? Modern philosophy emphasizes: *things that occupy our experience of the world.*

There are very practical, commonsense reasons why we assume the things that occupy our experience of them are separate and distinct from our encounter with them. However, a moment's reflection, please, to realize the indubitable: *our only access to them is through our experience of them.*

On the one hand, we can be sure of the content of our own ideas and impressions. On the other hand, can we be certain of the source of our ideas and impressions? Out there? Are you sure? By what evidence?

5. I know, I know: *We are a people who get things done!* At every turn of daily life we are directed by common sense to accomplish a practical task at hand. And common sense insists on its pre-condition, the preconception that allows common sense to work: there is an *out-there* out there containing a matrix of physical entities located in space and time, causally interconnected.

Philosophy *vs.* common sense ... philosophy *and* common sense: what are their interests, their concerns? Can philosophy claim any practical result? Philosophy has a contribution to make about who and what we are but makes no contribution to our all-consuming commonsense pursuits. Indeed, from the commonsense perspective, philosophical investigation is an obstacle to accomplishing practical affairs.

Busy as we are with the ever-present task at hand, philosophy only distracts and gets in the way of practical business. Leisure, and the relief from the tedium of daily tasks, is a necessary pre-condition to allow intellectual pursuit.

Idle hands are the devil's workshop. Idle hands a mischief make. But listen to Bertrand Russell (*In Praise of Idleness*):

> **(Leisure) ... contributed nearly the whole of what we call civilization. It (leisure) cultivated the arts and discovered the sciences; it wrote the books, invented the philosophies, and refined social relations.**

6. There is trouble with language. For common sense the common vernacular will do, but philosophy has only the common vernacular to deal with disparate realms of speculations, requiring specialized vocabulary and new ways of thinking.

On one hand, the *existent* and on the other hand the *essential*: each requires its own specialized expression. Stretching ordinary language for each is difficult. Philosophy tries with talk about *The Particular* vs.

The Universal. But such talk uses up mental energy and is a distraction, an obstacle, when we are engaged in practical business.

Then, there's the *out-there*. Philosophy needs to ask, where is that? How do you know there is such a thing. (But, of course, the *out-there* is not a thing, and we cannot see it the way we see things we are certain are out there.) Common sense says *Oi vey! This is an inconsequential distraction.*

Engaged in commonsense purposes, we think of ourselves as separate and distinct from the world which is separate and distinct from the two oh-so-different ways—by the senses and/or by the understanding—that we access the *out-there*. On the one hand, the existence of things is at the fingertips of our physical senses ... seeing, touching, hearing, tasting, and smelling. And, too, we are familiar with how they work and what we need do to accomplish the next task at hand. Here common sense perks up.

On the other hand—and this is really where philosophy wants to go—there is the understanding that grasps essential nature, what is certain and universal ... the necessary truth of things.

For the purposes of operating in this realm of physicality, of course there is an *out-there* out there! Again, we are certain that the things which occupy our experience of them are fully constituted, fully real, separate and distinct from our experience of them.

Philosophical musing intrudes into this practical realm of happenings and doings with arcane, impractical, inconsequential distinctions and queries that disgust common sense as inconsequential to the business of accomplishing successful achievement.

7. Only you and I, no other beast, can distinguish the literal from the suggestive, the tangible from the insubstantial, the objective from the subjective; that is, what is *in-us* from the *out-there* that philosophy is

convinced is so far away from all that is *in-us*. (Yes, *in-us*; sorry, I don't have a better word for it.)

A note on speaking. We tend to think in oppositional dichotomies. It is not a point of philosophy, but perhaps of psychology, that the notion of *here* invites the rebound, the counter-point of *there*, of *not-here*. The notion of femininity invites the yin-yang reach for masculinity. The classical Art Deco wants to compare with the romantic Art Nouveau. Freshman art students, learning how to draw, practice how to (re)present things, objects, then the *negative space*, the *negative* entity (what a lovely oxymoron) constituted by the space surrounding and defining the object.

We think that our subjective awareness of things requires there to be an outside, an *out-there* to contain the things that cause our experience of them. We think it must be the case that the ideas and impressions (the content of which cannot be doubted) *in-us* establishes that there is—there must be—an *out-there* of things existing in a matrix of time and space and causality.

8. My view. I am convinced that the presence of masculinity in the absence of the feminine is a poor thing; you can neither say, nor think, what the positive means if there be no negative. But does the subjective certainty with which I bite into the crunchy red apple require that there be an objective crunchy red apple out there?

Again. I am certain, and there is no doubt about it: I see a red apple. Can I be likewise certain that there is an objective red apple out there causing what I see?

9. Thinking, as we do, of existence as an omnipresent and unavoidable intrusion upon the senses, then, of course, we must think there to be something intruding upon eye and ear. Rather begin here, says Berkeley. Begin with the question, *what does existence mean? What does it*

mean to say of a thing that it exists? The answer is non-controversial and indubitable: *Esse est percipi, To Exist is to be Perceived (or perceivable).*

What do you think? Is it indubitable? To exist does not mean to be an entity objectively constituted in space and time, ready to impinge its appearance on the senses. Be cogent and coherent in how you think and speak: synonymous existence and perception cannot be separated, require each other, stand ready to replace each other.

10. You think *existence* is out there. Berkeley suggests you try out this insight: By its *meaning*, existence is located in your perception. That is, you think the presence of things in your perception demands there be an *out-there* that houses physical things that cause your perceptions. But a fair-minded appraisal both confirms the content of your perception and, too, realizes that there is no warrant to think there is an *out-there* outside your experience of the world.

11. Does existence *exist?* Things exist. Existence is not a thing and does not exist. What is existence? Beware being fooled by the structure of language. Ask what is x? By the structure of language, we tend to think that whatever is x, it must be a thing. Uh-oh!

Berkely goes on to argue that we reinforce our commitment to the *out-there* by thinking that things are made of *matter*. But *matter*, whatever it might be, does not exist, is not a thing, but a commitment to material substantiality. A commitment based on ... what?

Things are made of *matter?* What does that even *mean?*

Out There, Part Two

Is there any knowledge in the world which is so certain that no reasonable man could doubt it?

Bertrand Russell, "Appearance and Reality," *The Problems of Philosophy.*

1. To a friend, The Father of Modernity, Rene Descartes writes: **My only access to the things out there is through ideas in me.** Before Descartes, philosophy always began with its concern about *things*. Philosophers call that traditional first branch of philosophy *metaphysics*, the investigation into the essential nature of things. (*Meta*, above, beyond, transcending... what, but *physis*, nature—from which we get our *physics*).

Descartes turned philosophy modern by re-directing its first attention away from things out there to our *experience* of things, to our own ideas of things, to our only access to things.

After all, we do not see their essential nature, and we do not see what is necessarily true about things. From its beginnings, and for more than a thousand years philosophy began with its metaphysical investigation into the nature of things. Then, Descartes.

So obvious in hindsight, so easy to see and say, but Descartes was the *first* to say *my only access to the things outside me is through the ideas inside me*. Want to know about things out there? Then you must begin with our access to things. Modern philosophy and psychology begin.

This Cartesian invention of modernity opens the door to the possibility of the grandest philosophical accomplishment of contemporary thought. First Descartes: Our access to things is undeniably prior to the things to which we have access. A century and a half later, the Father of Contemporary Philosophy, Immanuel Kant: *Does the nature of our access to things—the nature of our own ideas and the nature of our experience of things—determine the nature of the things we come to know?*

Before Descartes and Kant, philosophy leaps beyond our own ideas of things to the things themselves. Descartes and Kant, and then: *does the nature of our knowledge shape the nature of the things of which we have knowledge?* After all, to know by sight and to know by understanding are not the same thing.

2. To be modern and contemporary: Knowledge is prior to, and perhaps shapes the things we have knowledge of. Philosophers call this branch of philosophy *epistemology* (from the ancient Greek, *episteme* [say ep-is-stay-may], knowledge, understanding). Want to know about things? First, investigate the nature of knowing. After all, that is our only access!

Making philosophy modern, Descartes introduces—re-defines—ideas, not as objective re-presentations of things, but as mental events, personal possessions, and the only possible location for certainty. To be modern is to begin, not with things out there (outside your idea of them) but with your own ideas about things. Your own idea is your only access to them, and the only possible location for certainty. The content of your own ideas—about that you cannot be mistaken.

A fine entrée to modern thought: the search for certainty.

3. I can see the door. I can see that it is open. I cannot see what is *true* about doors. Nice question: the door is out there to be seen but where is the truth about doors? Nicer question: *what* is the truth about doors that I can know but cannot see?

Certainly, the truth about doors includes that to be a door means to function as open or as closed. So, the truth about doors is a *meaning*. Let me note that I can see the door; I cannot see its meaning. Let me note that all I see about the door is happenstance and circumstantial, and nothing certain. It happens to be open, or it happens to be closed, but I cannot see what it means to be a door.

I know what you are thinking. If I never witnessed a door-closing or a door-opening, then perhaps I would never come to know what it means to be a door. However, how you come to know the essential reality of things is not a question on the table. The truth remains undeniable: We cannot *see* what it *means* to be a door. We cannot see anything certain about *door-ness*.

For all of us, man and beast alike, things make an appearance, we can see what they look like. But man, and man alone, is the only creature that can know what is the essential reality of things, what is their essential truth.

4. Out there (wherever that is) are things, where is the truth of them? Out there? Of course not; truth is not a thing to be located somewhere, neither out there nor in me. Essential truth is a function of the accuracy of meanings. And you and I are the only creatures that discover, that create access to essential meanings.

A note in passing: *psychologism* is the common error of thinking that truth is a function of the mental event that thinks it; as though seven plus five equals twelve only if and when someone thinks it.

5. The world is a happening place. Out there is turmoil, circumstance, happenstance. Things out there seem like a random chaos of flotsam and jetsam pulled hither and dither by the tides of chance. Is the *out-there* real? Are things that occupy our experience of the world really out there?

I know, I know, the occurrence of events and circumstances seems to have specific cause(s), but the appearance things make to eye and ear is all purposeless and of no intention. The act of seeing contains no grasp of essentialness or necessity; so much for *seeing is believing*. And, let us note: no one has ever seen a cause.

6. Descartes' example. The tower I know to be square looks round from afar. The enormous statue atop a tall, tall pedestal looks small. Do I get anything but looks from out-there? After all, the sun looks to be about the size of a quarter. How can I trust to be true what a thing looks like?

Whales and dolphins lack the cones in the eye that permit color vision; they see in black and white. What do they see when looking at a red apple? Is it true that the apple which appears to be red is really red? Of course! But that's a truth about us, about how we see. There is no red in (better *on*) the red apple, but only this: a reflected wavelength of light that causes us to see it as red.

It seems to me that there is an *out-there* out there that is needed to house the things that seem to be out there. Is h*ow it looks to me* enough to say how *it is*? If there is an *out-there* out there, there is certainly no certainty out there. Are you certain there is an *out-there* out there?

7. The search for certainty is the hallmark, the bellwether, at the beginning of every serious philosophic inquiry since the Father of Modern Philosophy, Rene Descartes, invented the modern way doing

philosophy with his insight as to what is undeniably certain. Certainty can be found only in our own ideas.

Certainty. I think, and I think it is certain that the *I think* proves there is—must be—an *I* to do that. My thoughts are, well, mine, indubitable, and prove that *I*, as thinker, *I* am a *self*; proof that *I am*. Can any of this be denied?

Modern philosophy is underway in its search for certainty; modern psychology begins, is initiated by the Cartesian redefinition and emphasis on ideas as mental events, as our own personal possessions, not just an objective (re)presentation of something.

I am ... what? A self-conscious, reflective intellect, a thinking self, possessing and being possessed by my own ideas, adventitious and otherwise. Descartes, the Father of Modern Philosophy, is as well the Father of Psychology.

Believe it or not, Descartes invented our modern notion of *idea*. Before Descartes, everyone thought an idea to be objective, like our notion of the ideal. A good idea was an accurate, well done, objective representation of a thing. Homer presented a very good idea of what is a hero, and offered exemplars of heroism in Achilles and Hector. A good idea of something was a good representation of its essential nature.

8. Then comes Descartes and the modern focus, not on the objective idea-as-representation, but on idea-as-certain! Again, we cannot doubt the content of our own ideas. Again, ideas-by-sense, by their very nature, are always open to doubt. Ideas based in the innate operation of the understanding is the only location for certainty. And modern thought begins.

I am a thinking thing! Thinking makes me to be! That is, *I think*, therefore *I am*. In Descartes' French, *Je pense, donc je suis*. Now—to avoid the so pervasive error in so many introductory textbooks—I am ...

what? An *existing* thing alongside all the *existing* things out there? The Cartesian foundation for modern philosophy is not *I think, therefore I exist*. No, *I am*, when and only when, I am thinking. *I am a thinking thing*. Rationality is my being. And rationalism is the first school of modernity.

Existence refers to things we suppose to be out-there, things that we bump into, see, hear, feel, smell and taste. There is no necessity, no certainty concerning existing things that occupy my sensed experience of the world. The whole realm of existence is suspect, circumstantial, happenstance. This skepticism is a hallmark of modernity.

9. Again, before Descartes, philosophy began with the *things*, and how to understand their nature, what it means to say they are real. The revolution of Cartesian modernity: Ever since Descartes, philosophy begins with our own *experience* of things.

We are all Cartesian now. I cannot be mistaken that I am thinking about an elephant, but surely, I can be mistaken as to whether what I am thinking is true of elephants, or caused by an elephant, existing or not...correct?

10. From modernity to contemporary (post-1800) thought: Is thinking determined by the things I think about? Or, are the things I think about determined by the nature of the language in which I think?

That is, we think that *what* is first: reality, already constituted, prior to our arrival and making invitation for us to encounter it. That's the ordinary view, and seems logically compelling. After all, you cannot talk about something that is not, first, there, in front of you, inviting conversation.

I believe that first is the language in which we think. Language is prior to the things we think about and speak about, which allows us access to the world. Language allows us to intend the essentialness of things-seen. It determines and reveals the meaning and significance of the things we think about.

Here, my editor, Pat Regini asks, *When you say the language IN which I think, do you mean the language WITH which I think* (that is, do you mean the way the subject/predicate structure of categorical assertion in any language)? *Or do you mean, say, French or Italian or Swedish?*

Both!

11. No one has answered the question so succinctly as Saint John:

> *In the beginning was the word, and the word was with God, and ...*

(wait for it ... St. John goes on to define the Lord ...)

> *The word was with God. And the word was God* (!)

John wrote in the ancient Greek that uses **logos** for our **word**, from which we get our *logical*.

That is, God is **The Word.**

There is reason to believe that in proper logical order, language precedes, intends and reveals and and brings to light the essential reality of the world. This against the conventional view that prior and primary and first is an already constituted world inviting language to talk about it. That is, we think there first must be mountains and monkeys making themselves available for our experience of them. Them first, so that we know what we are talking about.

Evidence? You can see mountains and monkeys, but you cannot see what it means to be a mountain or a monkey. What it means to be a mountain or a monkey is an understanding you must bring to your encounter with those things. And that meaning remains hidden behind the appearance of mountains and monkeys until and unless you project, intend what those things mean; those things that occupy your experience of the world.

12. Out there, wherever that is, is a world to be revealed. You are a person empowered by language to render the world intelligible. You have the power and the responsibility. I think the world awaits you.

Out There, Part Three

1. We are equipped to access the world with *eyes to see* the things we think are out there, and too, with the *understanding to know* about the things we see.

We take it that our subjective experience of things is triggered by and confirms the objective reality of the things we see, and, too, the things we understand.

No doubt about it. Of course, things occupy our experience of the world, and they seem to be out there. *Out-there*. Where's that? Out where?

2. The power of language! Language does not simply name the things we see and describe how they look and how they work, but shapes and channels this or that way to think about things and understand them.

The power of language! Different sort of language, different understanding! Does an already constituted world, unaffected by our thinking and speaking about it, invite language to talk about it? Or does language intend the world in that way linguistically revealed?

We think the former. We think that things come first, are objective and fully constituted and prior to language which follows behind trying to catch up by naming things and describing their circumstance.

Reality is, we think, prior and previous and a condition of possibility for language, a secondary phenomenon, so to speak, that catches up and sticks names on things.

That's how we teach our children. *That's a truck, that's a car, that's Mommy.*

3. If it has a name, we think there must be a thing, an entity, a something, *so* named. That's the only evidence for our notion that there is an *out-there* out there! Correct?

I know, I know: you are so certain of the objectivity of the out-there, outside our subjective experience of the world. And, you are sure, an objective reality outside your experience of it is—must be—the cause of your experience.

The revolutionary, visionary, Irish co-instigator of modern philosophy (together with the Frenchman Rene Descartes) disagrees! We will look at George Berkeley's reasoning in a moment.

4. First this. Maybe it is the other way around. Maybe language is first, prior to and indicator of the reality that we must first understand so to become able to intend it and encounter it and bring it to light.

No *out-there* out there? Seems impossible! It seems silly to imagine there is no *out-there*. I know what you are thinking. The apple I eat, the chair I sit on, the wife I kiss, all are, if not out there, where?

I know what you are thinking. *I know there are apples and chairs and my wife. I can speak of them, describe their circumstance. What more proof do you want? Seeing is believing, being able to speak of things convinces that there are those things to speak about. And where are they? Don't be silly; of course, they are out there. They must be somewhere; if not out there, where?*

5. Called *the most original mind in modern physics,* Richard Feynman (Albert Einstein Award, 1954, Nobel Prize in Physics, 1965) said this about teaching physics:

> *It is my task to convince you not to turn away because you don't understand it. You see, my physics students don't understand it ... That is because I don't understand it. Nobody does.*

What could he mean? Our common vernacular is weighed down, loaded with unspoken, unthought preconceptions, shaped by our experience of the world, this world that we take for granted as being out there. We learn to speak of things in the closed in and prejudiced familiarity of common sense, of day in and day out interaction with things. We see and hear them; *they must be out there to be seen and heard.*

We learn to speak of things, for everyday common-sense purposes, and under common sense pre-conceptions (like there's really an *out-there* out there, containing fully constituted, fully real existing things unaffected by how or whether we know about them or not). *But does how we speak of them determine the nature of our experience of them?*

6. This speaking, together with it's taken-for-granted denotation and connotation, will not do if we are to be able to say—to think—anything sensible about Feynman's special interest, the structure and working of the atom.

We cannot talk cogently and coherently about the atom using the language with which we talk about our common experience of the world. But we must try; how else to describe the swarm of electrons *orbiting* about their sun, their nucleus. But Feynman says that's just a misunderstanding. Planets orbit the sun by gravitational attraction; no gravity inside the atom; rather electrons and their nucleus are in an electro dynamic tension. Feynman's work is called quantum electrodynamics.

Planets orbiting the sun is a gravitational structure; the theory of gravity makes no explanation of the innards of the atom which is a complex of quantum electro dynamics. But that electrons are *orbiting* is the best we can do with the common vernacular.

What are electrons doing and why? Feynman says he does not know; he cannot say, and the Noble Prize-winning advance he made in quantum mechanics relies not on words, not on mathematical formulae, but on a visual mapping design.

7. Perhaps language is not topic neutral. Perhaps what we talk about, what we think about, is of a type and a shape that requires its own shapely language. Too romantic a notion?

Shocking to common sense, but to be considered: Perhaps first comes the language that then, by its nature and character, allows us to speak about things appropriate to the language fit to reveal them.

Example. **These woods are lovely, dark and deep; But I have promises to keep; And miles to go before I sleep**, says Robert Frost. Can this serious insight into what it means to be human be said in any but poetic language?

8. The common vernacular is a language of things as they occupy our experience of the world. And atoms, along with their neutrons, protons, and electrons are *not* things. As to the things that occupy our experience of the world, perhaps the common vernacular is not the best language, even if it is required by common sense.

Whatever the atom is, it is not a thing, we cannot experience it, and it cannot be easily talked about in the way we talk about apples, chairs, or my wife. In everyday speaking, we talk about things we can bump into; no one ever bumped into an atom.

Ever bump into an *out-there*?

9. You can experience an apple, a chair, my wife. There is no experience of *out-there*. Don't you suspect that intelligent talk about *out-there* requires a special language, as a discussion of the objective nature of the atom requires its special language? And who knows what surprise might come if we could speak of the *out-there* in the language fit to speak of it.

The skeptical tone here is struck by the father of modern philosophy, Rene Descartes, who writes to a friend:

> **My only access to what is outside me is through ideas inside me.**

Everyday speaking does not know but assumes the *out-there*. We think: *How else to explain what is in us?*

10. In me are my ideas, impressions, imaginings, hopes. I know them. I am certain. Provocative modern philosophy: *I cannot be incorrect about my own ideas and impressions.* Provocative George Berkeley: *I think my thoughts are tied to things out-there, but is there any evidence for that?*

And are my ideas and impressions true? Descartes' example: The tower I know is square appears round from afar.

Does it make sense to ask if there's an *out-there* out there? I am convinced that things are out there. And, by golly, I am one of those things, asking about things that are, I think, out there. But what is the evidence for that?

11. Another question: If there are things out there, why are they? Why are there things? It is very possible, is it not, for there to be no things? I know what you are thinking. *If there were no things, then there would be no you, and no one to ask,* Why are there things?

I think that is correct, but does this truth make any evidence for positing an *out-there*?

This is an annoying reflection. You are thinking: *Of course there are things out there! They exist! You see them, bump into them, hold them, move them, smell them. They exist!*

12. Do space and time exist? Not like apples and chairs ... correct? You can eat an apple, sit on a chair; can you do anything like that with space and time? For that matter, does it matter that *matter* does not exist in the same way that material things exist?

Does matter exist? What exists has shape and color ... correct? What color is *matter*?

And you are certain that material things are made of, as Berkeley points out, this mysterious *matter*. Berkeley waits for some cogent and coherent explanation of this inexplicable *matter*.

And, for that matter, *matter* does not *not exist* in the same way that space and time do not exist ... correct? After all, matter is *stuff* ... correct? Space and time are specifically the absence of stuff.

13. The above is a general introduction to philosophical reflection, and a specific introduction to the rise of modernity in eighteenth-century France and Germany's Age of Reason, and England's Enlightenment.

Of what can we be certain? This is the question that begins every serious philosophical discussion since philosophy grew up and became modern.

We can be certain about the content of our ideas, that they are as I live them. This certainty cannot be doubted: that *I think* proves that *I am*. Descartes is careful in his meaning: I *am a thinking thing; I am* when I *think.* Whatever doubt is possible about the things out there, outside my idea and impression of them, this discovery of the self, what we now call the ego, is Descartes' first undeniable certainty. It is certain: there must be a me to host the ideas I live.

As he says in the Second Meditation:

> *I am, I exist, that is certain. But what then am I? A thinking being ...*

(Let us notice what's first, *doubts,* and last and least, *perceptions*)

> *... which doubts, understands, conceives, ... affirms ... denies ... rejects ... imagines ... and which perceives.*

> Rene Descartes, *Discourse on Method* and *Meditations.* Bobbs-Merrill, 1960.

This modern philosophy, with its Cartesian Subjective Turn and keenly honed skepticism, prepares for Immanuel Kant's invention of contemporary philosophy. That is, with this undeniable argument and persuasive method, contemporary thought offers: *Our thinking and how we think precedes and makes possible what we think about; intelligibility precedes and reveals reality.*

14. Review. In the new and innovative, modern mode of doing philosophy, Berkeleyans insist: *Only this can I confirm with certainty: my own impressions (and ideas). Things out-there ... cause(!) ... my impressions ...*

The Scotsman, David Hume, Berkeley's successor and titular leader in the English-speaking world to the modern movement, asks, *has anyone seen a cause? ...*

I know there are practical reasons why that's what you cannot help but think, but how do you know that? Berkeley thinks: *How is it that your knowledge goes past your impression of a thing to the idea of a thing out-there that causes what you see?*

Yes, things seem to be out there. That they really are is a notion you cannot defend. Then your intuitive sense (urged and directed by the pressure of practical day-in and day-out business) has the audacity to posit causes that are *out-there* alongside material entities that you suppose are *out-there*.

Be fair! Show me that all this is not a bunch of hocus-pocus you made up just to feel comfortable about how the world appears, about how the world looks to you.

The supposed cause and matter that you depend on to explain your experience of your world: are they really there, *out-there*, or do you suppose them to be out there only because you need them to render your sensible experience comfortable, cogent and coherent?

> *And here are trees and I know their gnarled surface, water and I feel its taste. These scents of grass and stars at night, certain (that) ... all the knowledge on Earth will give me nothing to assure me that the world is mine. You describe it to me and you teach me to classify it. You enumerate its laws ... At the final stage you teach me that this wondrous and multicolored universe can be reduced to the atom and that the atom itself can be reduced to the electron. All this is good and I wait for you to continue. But you tell me of an invisible planetary system in which electrons gravitate around a nucleus. You explain this world to me with an image. I realize then that you have been reduced to poetry ... that determinism are enough to make a decent man laugh.*
>
> Albert Camus, *"An Absurd Reasoning"* in *The Myth of Sisyphus and Other Essays*.

To be sure, you have that impression, but how do you defend the conjuring of a material entity, out there, *causing* it? We convince ourselves that existence refers to an objective material world outside and external to our internal undeniable idea of it. Why? The culprit, I believe, is common sense which must have an *out-there* filled with things to manipulate.

Berkeley: Is either meaningful (existence, perception) with a denial of the other? Or do they imply and demand and stand synonymously ready to replace each other? An impossible notion: an existing physical object, but not perceivable.

15. Dear reader, what is your fair estimate? Is Berkeley's **to be is to be perceived** undeniably correct? And is it correct that there is no warrant to suppose that the being of a thing requires material presence? Also unwarranted: our common and common-sense notions of *cause* and *matter*. To say of anything that *it exists*, what could that possibly mean other than it is perceived … or perceivable? And, again, there is no cogent, coherent meaning in any claim that matter is perceived or perceivable.

But—and clearly—that does not defend our made up, concocted view about the world that we think to be *out-there*, made up of *material* things which *cause* our impressions.

Again, dear reader, with your fair-minded estimate of Berkeley's astonishing but undeniable challenge: to say of anything that *it exists*, what could that possibly mean other than *it is perceived,* or is perceivable?

Our conventional, but indefensible, view about the world, out there, made up of things which, in turn, are made up of *matter*, which in turn *cause* our impressions. Perhaps we must take a closer look at George Berkeley—just in case his argument is as undeniable as it seems.

Berkeley flavors his (I think undeniable) view with the delicious *First we raise a cloud of dust, then we complain we cannot see.*

Oh, yes, perception brings impressions. Are those subjective impressions necessarily of some material object that exists *out-there*, outside in the inner subjective realm of mental activity? Other than the demands of common sense, by what evidence do you know that?

If Berkeley is correct, then objective existence and subjective perception are equivalent and make a linguistic distinction with no material (pardon the pun) difference. Each meaningful only in terms of the other, and that makes supposed objectivity conflate to subjectivity.

Oh, the modern! Subjectivity is primary. Ideas of things are prior to, and determinative of, the things they are ideas of.

16. No one has so formidable an impact on the method, means, results and consequences of modern thought than George Berkeley. I want to call modernism *Berkeleyianism*. Since Berkeley, we moderns know how to do it. Do not ask *What is it?* Ask *What does it mean?*

Obviously, if absent language and absent meaning, then absent reality! So exciting, so romantic a notion. Can it be denied: *It exists* means *it is perceived*? By what reason? The objective world is not a far distance from our subjective sensibility, but rather, we participate in the reality of the world by knowing it.

Only the letter 'L' (for *lovely reality*) separates the *word* from the *world*.

17. Seeing the world is not an add-on mechanism to a prior objective world waiting to be seen or not. The very act of perception of things is what it means that those things exist!

I would hasten to add: we participate in the reality of the world through our experience of it, both by the senses, and, also, by the understanding.

Indeed, through the understanding we reveal essential reality that otherwise remains hidden behind sheer, brute physical appearance.

"*It is*" means "*I can see it.*" "*I can see it*" means "*it is.*" Existence is meaningful, not as the substantial presence of material objectivity (for which there is no evidence) which is located somewhere out there, outside of subjective perception. Existence is a function of perception. Perception is a function of existence. So modern! So Berkeleyan!

Now the clincher! The *pièce de résistance*. What warrant, what reason, what evidence can claim that what I see is caused by an objective material physical object located *out-there*, outside my ken?

18. Dear reader, the world waits for you to know it. Shirk that uniquely human responsibility and essential reality remains hidden, silent, dormant and inert, behind the brute physical appearance available to all sentient creatures.

I Have an Idea

That an idea is subjective, yours, a mental event, is a brand-new notion, invented by the Father of Modern Philosophy (and psychology) in the early 1600s.

In Greek, *eido* (*I see it*) with the uncomplicated understanding that what you see is determined by the objective reality of what you are looking at.

> *The word 'idea' is now at home in ordinary language; but it is a word, like 'quality' and 'intention,' that was once a philosophical technicality. Its modern use derives, through Locke, from Descartes; and Descartes was consciously giving it a new sense. Before him, philosophers used it to refer to archetypes in the divine intellect: it was a new departure to use it systematically for the contents of the human mind.*
>
> Kenny, Anthony. *Descartes: A Study of His Philosophy.* St. Augustine,1968.

1. Believe it or not, Descartes (1596-1650) was the first to say this. Before Descartes *idea* meant what we mean by *ideal*. Idea *re*-presented that which it was an idea of, objectively, and with as much accuracy and insight as possible. A good idea was true to the thing it *re*-presented, not subjective but objective and splendid if accurate with much insight.

The idea of Achilles was the sublime portrait of a hero, so well presented in the Iliad and orally passed on over generations, so every new listener learned what it meant to be heroically Greek. Post Descartes, the idea of Achilles is a personal reflection, what and how you think of him. How modern.

2. It is very Greek to seek the best possible example of a thing: its archetype. How could you better know a thing than knowing its best possible example? So, from its beginning, philosophy finds *existence* problematic. The best possible one, its ideal, the definitional idea of it, does not—cannot—exist in the physical world where everything is bumped and bruised, ages and perishes.

The *best possibility* is not a whim but significant as the plan for the existing instantiations it inspires. The *best possibility* must *be* ... somewhere. Perhaps there is an upper realm, a heavenly ideal realm, where the best possibilities are contemplated by an omniscient God; an all-powerful God who, thinking the best possibility, cannot help but inspire it to (be)come.

The Greeks did not say that. Plato's heaven is not run by a god, but by the dynamic power of *The Good*. Enter the first full-blow western philosophy, its eyes looking up to the realm of perfection, of the *Forms*. How does Plato know that? How else to explain the source and origin of our existing world?

3. Descartes writes to a friend, **I am certain that I can have no knowledge of what is outside me except by means of the ideas I have within me,** and modern philosophy begins. Descartes is known as the *Father of Modern Philosophy*, and, too, of psychology and our contemporary notion of the self as a self-reflective thinking being.

4. Descartes' *Subjective Turn*, and now: *I have an idea. Of what? Nothing? Not possible.* An astonishing insight: the world occupies our idea of it!

And our idea of it is our only access to it. A contemporary step past Descartes: Our thinking and speaking shapes, forms, colors, and flavors that which we think and speak about. Descartes' discovery of the self as a thinking thing makes this grand contemporary insight possible.

The grandest insight of contemporary philosophy (*Intentionality*): *How you think and how you speak determines what you say and think about.* A favorite example: *These woods are lovely ... But I have promises to keep and miles to go before I sleep.* This can only be said and made understandable in poetic language. The language you speak, its nature and structure, determines what you are able to think and speak about.

This so modern insight corrects the ordinary view that the things we experience determine our experience of them. A whole new way to understand our unique responsibility: *our experience of it determines reality!*

5. Although it seems that objective reality and subjective awareness of reality are diametrically opposed, each of a nature denied by the other, there is philosophical reason to believe that their seemingly contrary natures, the subjective versus the objective, not only imply but infer and require each other! Either without the other: an empty concept and of no significance.

Time to write down your thoughts: *Does how-you-understand-the-world determine the world that you understand?*

It is modern to think that thinking defines us. It is modern to recognize that the objective world we encounter through the senses, and think about with the understanding, is available only through our own ideas, our own experience, our own encounter with it. Therefore, the objective world is a complement of our own subjectivity. The objective world, and, our own subjective experience of the world: moments of each other. Oh! So contemporary. So romantic!

6. First the century and a half debate of Descartes' modernity: Is our access to the out-there by the impressions gathered in by the senses as argued by empiricists, or by the ideas formed in the understanding as argued by the rationalists?

There is no avenue to the objective world other than these two subjective roads: the physical senses and the understanding. This is the great debate of modernity. Is knowledge by the immediate and direct vivid and vivacious inexorable flood of appearance into eye and ear? Is knowledge informational and happenstance? Or, is knowledge intentional as the understanding reaches out to things and apprehends what is necessarily and essentially true of them?

I know what you are thinking. *How can it be both?* Each brings a world utterly alien to the other. Every aspect and character of one (senses or understanding) is specifically denied by the other.

This debate, empiricist vs. rationalist, rages for more than a century, and then a remarkable solution.

7. Since my ideas and impressions are subjective, *in me*, far removed from the objectivity *out there*, it is modern to ask: *Which ideas are true? Do my ideas come from the senses or are they shaped by reason and intended by the understanding? Do my ideas reflect reality? Do they shape my knowledge of reality? How does subjective access to objectivity work?*

8. The empiricist answer from the English Enlightenment modernist John Locke: **Nothing is in the intellect that wasn't first in the senses**. The debate rages across the channel with the continentals who argue the rationalist view from their Age of Reason.

From the romantic continental rationalists: *Rationality is what make us to be human, and to be human is to reach for the excellent, the sublime, the essential and necessary truth of things.*

These ideas are unique to what it means to be a person, and available to no creature but us. Rationalism is convinced: True and significant ideas are innate, a priori, and necessary. (I take this tri-part description from John Cottingham's *The Rationalists* and His *Rationalism*.) Against empiricism, rationalism argues that knowledge is more than a familiarity with the sensed world, truth is more than how things happen to look. The truth of things requires apprehension of their essential nature, of what is necessary, not mere appearance of happenstance.

9. Do you know the red chair is a chair because it is red? Of course not! Guess, dear reader, where I stand on this debate. I know, you are on the other, empiricist side as are most English speakers. This ever since that view is so forcefully and elegantly elaborated in the English Enlightenment by the Englishman John Locke and Scotsman David Hume.

10. Ironically, the first English Cartesian, John Locke (1632-1704), answers Descartes question (*which of our ideas grasp the true of reality?*) in the very British, very empiricist, very anti-rationalist, anti-Cartesian,

> *No man's knowledge here can go beyond his experience.*
>
> Locke, John. *An Essay Concerning Human Understanding.* Hackett, 1996.

> *Let us suppose the mind to be, as we say, a tabula rasa, void of all characters, without any ideas. How comes it to be furnished? Whence comes it by that vast store, which the busy and boundless fancy of man has painted on it, with an almost endless variety? When has it all the materials of reason and knowledge.*
>
> Locke, John. *An Essay.*

Modernity! Now our own ideas are primary, and make access to the world, either by the senses, or to so different a world, by the understanding. So different a knower, if, as argued by the empiricists, proper access to reality is by the senses, or, on the other hand, as argued by the rationalists, the world is rendered intelligible by the understanding.

Which world do you live in? The world so vivid and vivacious as color and sound, smell, and taste flood into us? That is, the world received by the senses? Or, do you choose your world-experience by the opposite vector, from us to the world, and by the understanding which must reach out to and intend its intelligibility and apprehend what is necessarily true of things?

11. Empiricism does nest comfortably in classical English speaking and thinking. By its nature, empiricism wants verifiable fact. But rationalism flows with linguistic ease in romantic French and German. It is almost true that the flavor, tone and timbre of our linguistic elocution goes far to determine the tone of the world so determined.

With no side giving way on either side of the English Channel, the debate rages for more than a century. Empiricists argue that which occupies the world and occupies our experience of the world are known by sensible familiarity. The world and knowledge of it is experiential, factual, empirically verifiable, brought by the senses and constituted by appearances.

Empiricists think that necessity is tautological, true of words and their meanings as in *All men are mortal* and in *All bachelors are unmarried.* Tautologies, though, do not reveal the world. They are non-existential, non-informative, non-significant, irrelevant to the direct and immediate encounter of the world by eye and ear.

Speculation of what is necessary makes no contribution to the coming development of the new science based as it is on observable and verifiable fact.

Rationalists are certain that the measure of knowledge is certainty, and necessity cannot be apprehended in the flux of sensible experience. Truth is innate in the mind, deeply rooted in the structure of the understanding, and a priori (prior to) and explicator of the world reported by eye and ear.

So contrary, the empiricist versus the rationalist view. You may think that each determines the same world understood differently. Are they different worlds, one known empirically, and the other known rationally? I think the latter.

I know. You think—and you are certainly correct—that each, empirical sensing, and, too, rational grasp of essential truth has a role to play in knowledge. But if they combine ... how? Surely knowledge needs both the senses and the understanding. But they so oppose each other, the debate seems unresolvable.

12. The solution comes in the 1780s by the Prussian, Immanuel Kant in philosophy's grandest achievement, the realization that both empiricism and rationalism are *asking the wrong question* and *applying the wrong method*. The task is not to choose the correct path we take to the world, through the senses or through the understanding, but to ask of the world *how to understanding that knowledge is possible?*

Kant calls it his *Copernican Revolution*:

> **Hitherto it has been assumed that all our knowledge must conform to objects. But all our attempts to extend our knowledge of objects by establishing something in regard to them a priori, by means of concepts, have, on this assumption, ended in failure. We must therefore make trial whether we may not have more success in the tasks of metaphysics, if we suppose that objects must conform to our knowledge...**
>
> Kant, Immanuel. Critique of Pure Reason. Hackett, 1996.

Here the contemporary philosophical insight that subjectivity (our own ideas as access to the world) and objectivity (the world we make access to) are in no tension of opposition. They are moments of each other, requiring each other, inaccessible and empty of meaning in the absence of each other. *A love affair:* the objective world, and our subjective apprehension of reality.

We become who and what we are as knowers of the world. An easier elocution: *The world that we know is a moment of our knowing it!* And therefore, *our experience of the world is a moment of the world.* We, who know the world, and the world that we know are *moments of each other*, necessitating and delineating and requiring each other.

And, too, *delighting in each other:* too romantic? Perhaps the delight is in the self-recognition that we become what we are meant to be when we know the necessary truth of things, and judge how excellently they achieve their essential nature.

The grand Kantian insight. We can only know of the world that which is knowable about it. The world we know participates in our knowing it by presenting its knowability. That is, the knowability of objects-known conforms to the demands of how we know. Things we know must present to the structure of our understanding what is knowable about them, if we are to know them. Whew! Better read that again ... and slowly.

13. Kantianism focuses contemporary thought on this: *The objective reality of a thing that we see and know must itself conform not only to the very structure of our own seeing, but also to the very structure of our own knowing!*

What it means *to see* is a nice metaphor for what it means to know. *Seeing* is an empty notion in the absence of *something-seen. Consciousness* cannot be empty. To know means to know *something*.

Someone says: *I am seeing. You are seeing what? Nothing, but I am seeing.* I say, *not possible.* Just as seeing cannot be empty of content, the consciousness that I am interested in is intentional by nature, intending the very intelligibility of the things that occupy our experience of the world.

Things participate in our knowing them. We can only know what is knowable about things. Knowable? What does that mean? Things are knowable in as much as they conform to the demands that the structure of understanding places before them. What a mouthful and mindful and should be read again, and slowly.

14. This goes against the ordinary, common usage of *consciousness*, consciousness-as-a-disposition, consciousness as everything from dreaming, to feeling happy or anxious. Such dispositions are not the consciousness I have in mind.

Kant's solution to the impasse between empiricism and rationalism triggers the revolution of contemporary philosophy and underlies philosophy done from Kant's time to now.

Let's read again, the grandest philosophical accomplishment:

> **Hitherto it has been assumed that all our knowledge must conform to objects ...**

(... either by the senses or by the understanding ...)

> **But all our attempts to extend our knowledge of objects by establishing something in regard to them a priori, by means of concepts, have, on this assumption, ended in failure ...**

(... for more than one hundred years there is no solution to the empiricist/rationalist debate ...)

We must therefore make trial whether we may not have more success in the tasks of metaphysics, if we suppose that objects must conform to our knowledge ...

> Kant. *Critique of Pure Reason.*

Time to test if it is true that *how* we know determines *what* we know, and how we know, determines our nature as knowers.

It is beyond a doubt that all our knowledge begins with experience. But although all our knowledge begins with experience, it does not follow that it arises from experience. Experience without theory is blind, but theory without experience is mere intellectual play. ... All our knowledge begins with the senses, proceeds then to the understanding, and ends with reason. There is nothing higher than reason.

> Kant. Critique of Pure Reason.

Again!

It is beyond a doubt that all our knowledge begins with experience ...

(... So far, the empiricist view is undeniable ...)

But although all our knowledge begins with experience, it does not follow that it arises from experience ...

(... Thus far, the rationalist view is undeniable ...)

Experience without theory is blind, but theory without experience is mere intellectual play. ... All our knowledge begins with the senses, proceeds then to the understanding, and ends with reason. There is nothing higher than reason.

Kant. Critique of Pure Reason.

15. Review. First comes modernity: Descartes raises our ideas as primary, prior to the things we come to know, and our only access to the world. Now the first question for modernity: *Which of our ideas are true, and why?*

Then the grandest philosophical accomplishment: Kantianism initiates the contemporary romance: we and our world are not isolates, but, as a matter of meaning, and concerning human understanding, (in)form each other. All contemporary philosophy begins with this Kantian moment.

My favorite philosophical insight: *How* you understand *determines* what you understand. *How* you understand the world *determines* the world so understood. Given that you are in the world, then, If I am correct, the understanding of who and what you are is determined by how you understand the world. Again—an astonishing notion—your understanding of the world determines who and what you are! Your understanding of the world is your understanding of yourself.

A recommendable contemporary view:

> ... [T]*he obvious fact that we cannot know reality independently of consciousness, and we cannot know consciousness independently of reality—to do so would be to meet the one and the other in isolation, which is an impossibility. We meet consciousness only as consciousness of something; and we meet reality only as a reality of which we are conscious.*
>
> Lauer, Quentin. *Phenomenology, Its Genesis and Prospect.*
>
> **One can approach it from the side of reality of which we are conscious, from that of consciousness we have of reality, or from the point of view of a contact between the two.**

Lauer. *Phenomenology.*

If we are to know what anything is...we must examine the consciousness we have of it; if this does not give us an answer, nothing will.

Lauer. *Phenomenology.*

16. Example of the contemporary view.

According to rationalism, space, time, and causality not only are, but must be, real; more real than the intelligibility they lend to the regular order of the world. But, argue empiricists, only things you can see, hear and touch are real. Space, time and causality are not things, not real, but constructs we foist onto our experience of the world to try to bring it to regular order.

The great empiricist, David Hume, argued that out-there is nothing more than a series of events. They are real, they are empirically verifiable, as would say any good empiricist. If that series of events, the first always preceding, the second always following in our experience, then we have an intuitive need to explain and exclaim that *cause* is a cement of connection between them.

However, there is no empirical evidence that there is—really!—any such a thing. Cause is not a *thing*; We can only see and hear *things*. Out there is nothing more than a regular—no exceptions—series of events. We inject our notion of *cause* into the sequence of events as an explanation of what we witness.

17. Kant faces and solves this terrible and seemingly unresolvable impasse. Is it not more persuasive that space and time – and causality, too – are neither real nor irreal, but rather are conditions of possibility that the understanding imposes upon things to render them knowable?

Is it not more persuasive that things must present themselves to sight and intelligence as though they are spatially and temporally located and in causal connection, else we cannot know them?

18. Could there be (real) things but not in space and time, and not in causal connection? Logically possible. However, we do not, and could not, know about such a thing. We can only speculate about such possibilities, which we just did.

What, then, to say and think about space and time and causality? *Real? Irreal? Neither!* Neither *out-there*, nor *in-us*, but conditions-of-possibility, inherent within the structure of the mind, imposed by the understanding upon anything ... any thing ... that, then, becomes possible for us to know.

To be seeable, to be knowable, things must appear to us to be in space, in time, appear to us as though they really are in causal connection! To be sure, there could be things outside space, time and the chain of causality—but, then, we could not know them.

Knowability

1. Our favorite certainty, our most cherished belief about who and what we are, and how we know the world: *Seeing is believing.*

Is what we see what we know? Is what we know derived from what we see?

Seeing is passively and helplessly receptive of the appearance things make to an accommodating eye. Knowing is pro-actively accomplished by the engine of the understanding which grasps and renders intelligible the essential reality of things.

I know her! Oh, the ambiguity. Perhaps she is a casual acquaintance, and I am mildly and mechanically aware of what she looks like. Or do I know her accomplishment and achievement as a person?

English does not have the very fortunate French distinction between *savoir*, familiarity, and *connaitre*, the thorough grasp of a thing's inherent and intrinsic reality. *Savoir* is knowing how to do something; it is familiarity through repetitive exposure; *connaitre* is to know deeply, perhaps passionately; is knowledge of essentialness, not just appearance.

Oh, the ambiguity! I *know* how to tie my shoelaces: what the Greeks called *techne*, from which English derives its *technical*, but is that *knowledge?* All sentient creatures enjoy some level of *techne*, of skill. Both man and beast are aware of how things look and what they do, of happenstance, and how things work. But only man can know the essential, the necessary truth of a thing.

Do you want to say that the beast has knowledge because it *knows* how to do something? Or is it correct that only self-reflective, critically analytic consciousness can seek and understand and explain essentialness? No animal, only a person possesses the creativity made possible by the critical use of language.

2. Oh, the ambiguity! We say *know* to mean familiar, aware of how something looks, perhaps how it works. But that is not knowledge as in the understanding of a thing's essential nature. The most common, usual, conventional and mundane meaning: *She is familiar to me.* Familiarity is but awareness. All sentient creatures are, by definition, aware, however, that awareness, shared by man and beast, is not knowledge. Correct?

Awareness comes from, is formed and enhanced by a repetition of empirical experience with the appearance of things and is the cornerstone of environmental influence. Even the non-sentient flower shows its *awareness* by growing toward the light it needs.

The distinction here is between awareness and consciousness, best explained by Richard Mitchell in *Less Than Words Can Say:*

> **The speechless beasts are aware, but they are not conscious. To be conscious is to "know with" something, and a language of some sort is the device with which we know.**

3. So much for the pervasive conventional view that communication is the primary purpose and significance of language.

Listen to linguist Noam Chomsky (in a casual *You Tube* conversation):

One general assumption about language—almost a dogma—is that language is primarily a means of communication ... and it evolved as a means of communication. Probably that's totally false. Language evolved as a means of interpreting and creating thought. Yes, language can be used to communicate, but it doesn't seem that that is part of its design.

Chomsky, *Language and Thought*, You Tube. (Time: 4:49).

The startling insight that triggers contemporary philosophy: Things that occupy our experience of the world do not just become present by their appearance to eye and ear but participate in our knowing them by presenting what is knowable about them. Our knowing of them participates in establishing what they are! All this can be done through, and only through, self-reflective, analytical language—the uniquely human accomplishment.

All sentient creatures, that includes us, are in immediate and direct contact with the appearance things make to our physical senses. But only persons understand a thing's essential reality, and whether what we see and hear is happenstance or necessarily true.

Again, Richard Mitchell's marvelous insight:

The speechless beasts are aware, but they are not conscious. To be conscious is to "know with" something, and a language of some sort is the device with which we know.

4. *The very reality of a thing* cannot be seen and is not available in the physical appearance things make to eye and ear.

The very reality of a thin is its essential nature, hidden behind its physical appearance unless and until we intend it, render it intelligible through our appreciation of that essential reality.

Examples. Of course, the apple does not know what is apple-ness (what it means to be an apple), but, too, the dog does not know what is dog-ness. Only persons know, and that essentialness, apple-ness and dog-ness (and personhood) are revealed if and only if we inform our experience of things with our recognition and appreciation of their essential nature.

Apples and dogs are, in their existence, happy to fulfill what it means to be an apple, to be a dog, but only you and I know what that means. They exist, but what it means to be one of their kind does not and requires our intention to render their meaning intelligible.

We are uniquely able to intend. Only self-reflective persons, capable of understanding and apprehending a thing's essential nature can do that. If we do not understand and then intend, inform the meaning of them (in contradistinction to the existence of them) then that essentialness remains unrevealed until and unless apprehended and intended as an operation of the understanding.

The very reality of a thing can be brought to the light of understanding by, and only through, language. All creatures are aware of and interact with their physical environment. Only you and I can know, *really* know them; know what is *real* about them. And the only way to know this is by and through language.

5. Begin again. This time think of seeing as a metaphor for knowing. I think you will agree it to be undeniable: We can only see what is *seeable* about the thing-seen ... correct?

Then the shocker. What is seeable about the thing-seen is determined not by the thing, but by how our seeing works ... correct?

The thing-seen participates in our seeing it by presenting to us what we are able to see. Could it possess qualities that our vision is incapable of detecting? Of course. But whatever they might be, we cannot see them and cannot know them.

Surely, what we see is determined as much by how our seeing works as by the thing-seen ... correct?

Example. We see in color; whales and dolphins do not. So, color vision is as much the consequence of how our eye works as it is determined by the physical nature of colored things ... correct? This shows, doesn't it? that what we see is as much determined by how we see as determined by the thing seen.

Example. The red of the red chair, as basic science makes undeniably clear, is not in the chair, but in our own seeing the chair. The chair reflects the particular wavelength of light—which is not in itself red—causing us to see the chair as red. There is no red until lens, optic nerve and vision section of the brain bring us to *see* red.

Is it true that the chair is red? Of course. But this is a truth more about us than about the chair. There is no red in the red chair; where we see red is reflected light which is not red but of just the correct wavelength to cause what we see.

6. Think now of the mutual requirement between the world we know and we who know the world. Just as the thing-seen is a moment of our seeing, so is the thing-known a moment of our knowing!

We can only know what is knowable about a thing ... correct? What determines what-is-knowable-about-a-thing-known? What but the structure of the understanding through which and by which we are enabled to apprehend a thing's essential reality.

This is the core insight of my philosophical view. Known as *The Theory of Intentionality*: we can only know what is knowable about a thing. What is knowable about a thing ... ask your intuitive sense to wait for it ... is determined not by the thing but by the demand made by our own understanding. Whew!

7. Could something possess qualities or attributes that cannot be seen or known? I suppose so. But what can be said about such a possibility? Ah ... nothing! So, the thing seen participates in our seeing it by presenting to vision what vision is able to picture. Now, think about the thing-known.

Seeing and knowing cannot be empty. Seeing, to *be* seeing, must *be* seeing something; knowing, to *be* knowing, must *be* knowing about something. Seeing happens only in visible contact with the thing-seen; knowing is always—must be—knowing *about* something. Therefore, seeing and knowing are required moments of the thing-seen and the thing-known ... correct?

> *... [T]he obvious fact that we cannot know reality independently of consciousness, and we cannot know consciousness independently of reality—to do so would be to meet the one and the other in isolation, which is an impossibility. We meet consciousness only as consciousness of something; and we meet reality only as a reality of which we are conscious.*
>
> Quentin Lauer, Phenomenology: Its Genesis and Prospect.

What a becoming, lovely, romantic notion that illustrates the copulating intimacy between objective things-seen, things-known, proven to be required moments of our own experience, our own seeing and knowing! Whew!

Again, the thing-seen and the thing-known are required moments of seeing and knowing them ... correct? Seeing and the thing seen: two sides of the same coin; knowing and what is known: two sides of the same coin ... *n'est-ce pas?*

8. Knowing is always knowing about something. Knowing, about no thing, is no knowledge at all. Knowledge participates in the world known about by demanding that what we know conform to the structure of the understanding through which we know it.

With this insight Immanuel Kant initiates contemporary philosophy.

Whew! What a challenging, astonishing and, with enough open-minded reflection, undeniable realization that the objective and subjective—although conceptually distinct—are each meaningful only in logically requiring the other!

Begin historically here, in this philosophical revolution before Immanuel Kant [died 1805], with the birth, the invention of modern thought by Rene Descartes [died 1650]. Descartes writes to a friend: *My only access to the things outside me is through ideas in me.* Obvious to everyone before Descartes, *idea* was closely tied to, aligned with, and representative of whatever thing it is an idea of.

The idea of a thing shared the objectivity of the things it represented. Descartes builds the meaning of modernity on the notion that an idea is subjective, a mental event, a personal possession. Obvious and undeniable once said. Descartes was the first to say so.

9. Awkward in English, but a proper speaking of things in German, what is *knowable about them*, their *knowability*, is their *Bewuustsein*.

Could there be a reality beyond the reach of the understanding? Could there be truths beyond our ken? Could be, but what could you say about them? You could perhaps speculate and reason about such unknowable possibilities as, for example, the existence of God, but you cannot *know* them... correct?

Does God exist? Don't know. It is not decidable by the understanding. Let's be sure we understand that, when we pursue such a question, we are speculating and not dealing with what is knowable by the understanding when thinking about such an entity as God.

About God's existence we can speculate, reason with evidence oblique or direct. However, this is not a matter for the understanding, but speculative conjecture, and cannot be understood, but only reasoned about.

10. The major steps that lead to contemporary philosophy: First, Cartesian modernism distinguishes an idea to be subjective, a mental event, a personal possession. This is our modern notion of *idea*, a psychological event, distinguished from its historical meaning, something objective, representing an objectively real thing.

Historically, an idea was true by being true to the thing it represents, a notion closer to our *ideal*, the best and most beautiful picture of a thing. Now, with idea as a subjective mental event, the tone and timbre and major theme of modernism: *Which of our subjective ideas are true, and how do you know that?*

And now—for we moderns—the singular significance of such distinctions between fact vs. value; between that which is of necessity vs. happenstance; about the nature of the language in which we express the content of our ideas.

From Descartes to Kant the question is *Which of our ideas are true?* Empiricists say by ideas of sense, fed by the flood of appearance things make to eye and ear. Or, as rationalists say, by ideas generated in the innate operation of the understanding?

Kant declares ... *wrong question!* Philosophy does not begin as inquiry into the nature of knowledge already achieved. Rather, the question is: *How is knowledge possible?* The question is not, *How do we know?*—empirically or rationally—but, rather, *how is it possible that we know?*

11. Begin with the undeniable insight that what we know is limited to and contained within the parameters of *what is knowable*. Want to know about knowledge? Know that you are asking not about knowledge-already-achieved, that by its nature is empirical, received by the senses, or rational, constructed by the innate operation(s) of the understanding, but about *knowability itself*.

This knowability is presented to us by things as they occupy our experience of them. That is, the things that occupy our experience present their knowability on demand of the structure of the understanding, that, for example, insists that things seem to be, and present themselves as being located in space and time and causally enmeshed. And if they do not so seem, if they fail to conform to the demands of the understanding, then, alas, they are unknowable!

12. But space and time and causal connection are not *out-there*, like things we know seem to us to be out-there. Neither are space and time and causality in us. These are not things to be located outside us, nor are they mental events located in our experience of the world. These (space, time, causality) are conditions of possibility that things must meet if we are to be able to know them! These are conditions imposed by the structure of the understanding on things we think are *out-there*, that render things knowable. Whew!

Let's notice the intimate, mutual relationship between things-knowable-and-known, and the understanding that renders them knowable by intending their inherent and intrinsic essential nature. That which is known, and our knowing them: mutually requiring moments of each other; each empty and meaningless in the absence of the other. Whew!

Easier to say in German with its **Bewuustsein**, and with Germanic thinking, not factually about the world, **das Welt**, but transitively about the world-in-this-or-in-that-way-understood and with what we are prepared to know, with our worldview, our **Weltanschauung**.

13. To know (about) something is to know yourself knowing it. Too romantic a notion?

Sophistication

1. *Sophia,* a woman's name with an interesting etymological ambiguity. *Sophia,* ancient Greek for *wisdom,* as in *philo* (love); philosophy, love of *Sophia,* love of wisdom. But *sophia* is also the root of *sophistication,* to be clever and endowed with poise, panache and *sophistical* disingenuous use of language to deceive. The first philosophical debate that initiates western philosophy and western civilization: Socrates, advocate for *wisdom* versus the Sophist celebration of common sense.

2. Fifth century BC Greece sees the first institution of higher education. The sophists are the first professional teacherly class. For a fee they trained the sons of wealthy Greek families to *arete,* excellence. The Sophist definition of excellence: personal success. Life is a competition; the sophists trained their students in how to win in argument or debate, to convince others to their opinion.

Look around and recognize such sophistical tendencies today: pervasive skepticism of the attempt at objective truth that does not contribute to winning a more comfortable life.

Protagoras: *Man is the measure of all things.* That is, what is real and right is what those in authority feel is real and right.

Gorgias: *Nothing exists; even if something exists, nothing can be known about it; and even if something can be known about it, knowledge about it can't be communicated to others.*

3. Sophisticates are, well, cool and clever ... correct? *Are they wise?* Is it wise to practice and train to achieve sophistication? Is that the proper achievement for a person? But to that purpose the most prominent rainmakers, shakers, and king makers, the Sophists, the prized teachers of *arete*, of excellence, of Socrates day, trained the aristocratic youth to sophistication and so to achieve positions of success.

4. To be sophisticated is to abhor the honest, simple life. Unsophisticated is Henry David Thoreau's *Walden*. Intent on deploying God's original plan for us, the Amish way eschews such devilish enticements as electronic powered devices like television and telephones.

The sophisticate has *savoir-faire*, know-how-to-do, are worldly-wise, possessing poise and grace, elan and tact in dealing with life's delicate situations. The sophisticate works to gain status in the eyes of his fellows. He is dapper, elegant, and adept with sophistry that overwhelms his plainer fellows.

Sophisticates are cool. They do not follow the rules, they make their own rules, then, with finely honed sophistry turn others to their purposes. Sophistry, sophistication go together like hammer and nail; the sophisticate's success is a victory of sophistry.

Sophistry is the art of convincing to the weaker case. Think of television advertisements. The sophistical purpose is to convince us that, although logically irrelevant, we should surrender to sentiment and the intuitively comfortable. But the objective truth and how you feel about things have nothing to do with each other.

5. Socrates: *No! Stop! Enough! We are made not to be clever, but to reveal and appreciate the objective truth, whatever the cost to our easy impressions and favorite undefended beliefs.*

We are not made to just to find out how we feel about things, but to bring to the light of intelligibility what is good, true, beautiful, excellent, sublime.

We are not made to play the advantages and disadvantages that arise out of the shortcomings of others.

Well, then, what are we made for? Socrates answers: *The unexamined life is not worth living.* We are made to explore the question: *What are we made for?* No other creature, neither god nor beast, only man can and must do that in order to become what we are meant to be.

6. Socratic/Platonic idealism, the first fully developed philosophical view, triggers the beginning of western civilization with the question: *What does it mean to be a person? What marks us as unique and measures our ascendency above the beast? Sophisticated man, uniquely clever or the only sentient creature capable of digesting wisdom? The choice in every life: To be sophisticated and clever, or perhaps simple but wise?*

Sophisticated, wise, the same? **No**, *declares Socrates.*

The path to becoming a serious person is paved with the investigation into the question: *What does it mean to be a person?*

The Greeks know that, among all creatures, only we are required to make ourselves become what we are meant to be. The beast is born complete and needs only tribal guidance and environmental experience to achieve whatever is species determined. Survival in comfort and pleasure is the success well understood by the sophist.

But you and I are the only creatures that begin with unfulfilled potential. You and I are the only creatures tasked with the responsibility to choose who and what we may (be)come. Careful! We are the only creatures capable of malicious intent. We are the only creatures that can fail.

7. The Socratic cry is taken up anew by the contemporary existentialist. Choose! The life of the beast or, as urged by the gods, a serious life of higher purpose, driven by the search for wisdom. The devil tempts us to sophistication.

The search for wisdom ... about what? About what is not merely circumstantial and happenstance, but necessarily true and reveals the essential reality of things.

This reminds of George Orwell's *A good book tells you what you already know.* You already know, else there is no point and purpose of reminding you about the importance you place on what you happen to find attractive.

8. In the first great philosophical debate, at the very foundation of Western civilization, pudgy, fearless, gad-fly Socrates challenges the oh-so culturally successful Sophists, Protagoras, Gorgias, Hippias, and Thrasymachus. The Sophist's banner: All man has is his estimate of the real and the true. There is no real truth other than what is wielded by those in power. The Sophists: *The business of becoming a person is the business of succeeding to a position of power.*

The Sophists hired themselves out to tutor the aristocratic young of the Aegean-wide cosmopolitan federation of local autonomous independent city-states. Their goal: to teach the youth to get to the top, to get over their fellows by sharp rhetorical sophistry; to win the contests of practical life.

9. Plato's most famous metaphor: *As the light of the Sun illuminates, inspires, and makes possible our appreciation of the wonders to be explored in visual experience, so does the Good* (how-good-a-thing-is) *inspire things to be, to become in their physical existence as well accomplished and achieved as blueprinted by their definition, their essential meaning.*

Which will you choose to be? Idealist or a sophisticate?

High Moments

1. In every life there are ascending plateaus, each is a preparation for and must be accomplished before the next. From childhood to adolescence, from youthful and not yet developed adulthood to a self-reflective and deliberate maturity, each step up requires the step before. Then, alas, the decline.

In the history of western philosophy there are four high ... make that, highest ... moments. The first high moment is the *Idealist Beginning* with Socrates and Plato. The second moment: Aristotle's *Realist Rebellion*, a return from Platonic Idealism to the empiricist view—a respect for analysis of information gathered by the senses. This too, Aristotelian empiricism opens the West to the possibility of science.

Then, after two thousand years (the third highest moment), Rene Descartes raises philosophy out of its adolescence. For a century and a half, from the early 1600s to the late 1700s, western civilization feels and wears its Cartesian modernity. The Enlightenment in England and the Age of Reason on the continent, Europe then awakens to the promise of science.

It is the age dedicated to *progress* while, at the same time, a furious debate rages between the mostly English-speaking *empiricists* (*science and sense experience will unravel all our perplexities*) and *rationalists* (*certainty in knowledge can only come from reason triggering the understanding to apprehend what is necessary, not just happenstance*).

The most recent and most grand philosophical moment arrives with Immanuel Kant. Kant invents contemporary philosophy with his astonishing insight that *how* we know determines *what* we know.

Begin here, at the birth of the West with Socratic/Platonic *Idealism*. Then Plato's student, Aristotle, in a very adolescent-like rebellion, brings our civilization to *Realism*, with its invitation to investigate the nature of things on their own terms. Now empirical science becomes possible.

After achieving modernity with Rene Descartes and maturity with Immanuel Kant, philosophy turns left for a century and develops its romantic high moment with Karl Marx. And perhaps that is why (as I believe) philosophy must fall into its inevitable decline. These are the intellectual high moments in the growth of western civilization. Now the postmodern declination.

2. Plato's romantic idealism is founded on his invention of our modern notion of heaven as the upper realm of reality where resides potent necessary truth. Platonists look up to the realm of the divine as origin for and explanation of the mundane world we occupy in day-in and day-out living. The upper realm, the realm of the *Good*, the divine and most real, transcending and explaining the factual world is prior to and blueprints our mundane world of random and otherwise inexplicable physical happenstance and circumstance.

They appear to the senses, but appearances to the contrary, the appearance of the ordinary things of this mundane world are but shadows. Of what? Of their definition, of their meaning, of their *Form*. Their essential nature, their what-it-*means*-to-be-one-of-their-kind, cannot be seen, heard or experienced ... correct? We see and hear only individual, accidental, idiosyncratic and egocentric examples of an essential meaning ... correct?

According to Platonic idealists, the things that occupy our experience of the world are but instantiations of their *idea*—make that, *ideal*—of what they *mean*. Better ones are better examples. Can this be denied? Therefore, the *Good* is the measure of reality. And, therefore, the *Good* is more real than anything it judges to be a good example of its kind.

3. Thus far Aristotle must agree with his teacher, Plato. Reality is not what we *see*, but what we *know*. And what makes a thing that occupies our experience of the world to be real? Answer: *How good a one is it?* How well does it achieve what it was meant to be? How good an example is it of its essential nature? How close to its best possibility does it accomplish itself?

Aristotle: *But can we not adjudicate this achievement (or failure) in terms of its own physical state?* What need is there for an upper realm, origin of and inspiration for this day-in and day-out physical world in which we find ourselves? Can we not analyze how well accomplished things are *in their own terms?*

Do we *need* Plato's conjecture of a supreme and perfect *Good*, occupying an Olympic-like pinnacle in some hypothetical *upper* realm, separate and distinct from the inherent and intrinsic good that things accomplish in the life they lead in their physical state?

This is the first invitation to western science. *Let's discover what we can find out about things by examining them in their own terms.* And Aristotle goes on to invent biology.

Aristotle is factually oriented to our existing physical world and prepares the West for science.

4. Aristotle's *Correspondence* theory of truth held sway over the western world until Descartes' reformulation of the nature of our ideas. Aristotelian truth is a correspondence between what we say and think,

accurate to the world we think and speak about, unchallenged and unchanged for two thousand years. Then Descartes invents our modern notion of idea, a mental event, and true, indeed, certain, if our idea is so *clear* and *distinct* it cannot be denied.

Subject/predicate assertions that so-and-so is such-and-such are accurate or inaccurate to the substantial structure of things. Accurate reflection of the world? Then true. That's Aristotle and that is the western tradition for the next two thousand years.

The cat is on the mat is verified to be true, or false, by taking a look. In modern parlance, Aristotle is an empiricist, a realist determined to find out about the world in its own terms. Descartes is a rationalist and reason is the arbiter of truth.

5. Plato is an idealist. Our ordinary world is a shadowy thing inspired to be, to be(come). To be(come) as best it can, as close as possible—given the hardship of physical existence—to each thing's *Form*, definition, best possibility.

What's really real about things is their best possibility—what it *means* to be one of those things. Of course, that ideal, the full and perfect definition of things, can never be found here in this ordinary, mundane and bruised world. Therefore, there must be a heavenly (not Plato's word) realm of perfect *Forms* of things.

There must be a divine realm, as blueprint and template to explain the coming to existence of the mundane, ever-changing, bruised physical world.

The Platonic intuition is that, appearances to the contrary, the *Good* and the *Beautiful* and *Excellent* mark and measure reality. Platonists see past the appearance of things and ask, *How good a one is it? That's a beautiful one!* means that it is—really!—a real one.

6. After the Aristotelian moment, a large leap. Far distant is maturity from adolescence; two millennia from Aristotelian all-encompassing Realism to the civilized maturity of the Frenchman, Rene Descartes (Father of Modern Philosophy) and then the Prussian German, Immanuel Kant, inventor of contemporary philosophy.

Descartes writes to a friend: *My only access to the world outside me is through ideas inside me.* This is the origin of modern thought. Want to make inquiry about the world? Then you must begin with our access to the world. This revolution of proper method is known as *The Subjective Turn*.

So clear, cogent, and undeniable once you say it, but it took two thousand years for Descartes' grand insight which inspired modernity. Descartes invents the modern notion that an idea is not an objective re-presentation of the thing it presents, but subjective, a mental event, awaiting our self-reflective appraisal.

We moderns understand that my subjective idea is counterpoised against its objective content. And now, the problem for modernity: Which of my ideas and impressions are true of the world? Which of my ideas are dependable and true and which are contorted by the consciousness in which they reside?

Before Descartes, everyone who thought about it, thought an idea was something objective, dependent upon the object *idea-ed*, imaged, presented. An *idea* of something was our modern notion of the *ideal*, presenting its object in its best possible light. A good idea was true to the thing it denoted. A good sculpture or painting or picture or description of a thing was true to the thing it re-presented. Homer's Achilles and Hector are superb ideas of heroism.

Descartes' *Subjective Turn* turned philosophy modern. Now modern and a new set of terrible problems:

What to make of the difference between ideas that come from outside me and ideas that are innate?

By what method will we discover which of our ideas are true?

Are subjective ideas—mental events—reliable reports of objective reality?

Can the ever-changing flow of consciousness capture any certainty?

What am I?

Am I this physical body to which I have direct and immediate access through the senses?

Do my senses accurately report the truth of the things that occupy my experience of the world!

7. Traditionally, philosophy begins with *metaphysics,* the attempt to explain the reality of things. The insight that begins modern Cartesian philosophy: to find out about things we must first investigate our only access to things, namely our own ideas and impressions of them.

We cannot help but *see* the world and we want to *understand* it. Doesn't that suggest that we investigate subjective *seeing* and *understanding*?

With Descartes' insight into the primacy of our own ideas, metaphysical questions about the objective world must wait for epistemological conclusions about the nature of knowledge.

8. The Cartesian *Subjective Turn: The right way to find out about our world is to examine our only access to the world, seeing or hearing it, or on the other hand, understanding it,* prepares the way and makes possible the next plateau, contemporary philosophy.

First, the Cartesian revolution, the invention of modernity. The proper philosophical beginning to find out about our world is to investigate our only access to the world. Then, a century and a half after Descartes, Immanuel Kant brings his remarkable contemporary insight. To be modern is to begin our inquiry into our own access to the world. Then, the contemporary question: *Does how we access the world determine the world in that way experienced?*

Contemporary philosophy: Does *how* we see the world *determine* the world in that way seen? Does *how* we understand the world *determine* the world in that way understood?

9. Descartes' *Subjective Turn* is brought to full flower by Kant in the late 1700s with the modern and then contemporary recognition that our own experience of the world is a determining factor of the world in that way experienced.

That is, hidden behind the appearance physical things make to the senses is an essentialness that must be intended by the understanding if the world is to be revealed to the understanding. That is, we do not simply encounter a world already constituted and ready to be apprehended. Rather, our experience of the world shapes the way the world is apprehended!

10. The most handy entrée to contemporary philosophy: *We can know only what is knowable about the world. And what is knowable about the world is not determined by the nature of reality, but by the structure of the understanding which imposes demands concerning knowability on the reality to which it reaches out.*

We need examples. Consider the nature of space, time, and causality. Argue empiricists: These are not real things. Real things make sounds, are colored, shaped; you can see and hear them. What does cause sound like? What color is space? What shape is time? Rationalists insist that cause, space and time are not only real, but, so to speak, more real than the physical things they render intelligible. Absent cause, time, and space, the world implodes into chaos rather than into an ordered cosmos.

Kant: Cause, time, and space are neither nor irreal. They are conditions of possibility imposed by the structure of the understanding as a foil by which the world is rendered knowable. Things must present themselves to the understanding as though they are causally connected, temporally and spatially located, else the understanding cannot render them knowable.

Whew! A nice Kantian insight. Could there be things outside and irrespective of the understanding's need for things to abide by the rules and regulations concerning cause, space and time? That is, could there be things-in-themselves (noumena) that are real but outside the rules of behavior demanded by cause, space and time? Kant says: *There could be such things. But, we could not know them!* We can only know *phenomena*, things that obey the rules of causality, space and time, rules imposed by the understanding on any phenomenal thing.

11. Beasts and children simply see the world, and are locked into what they can use or enjoy. Only you and I can bring an understanding, an intention of what things mean, a knowledge of their value and whether, or not, they are well achieved examples of what it means to be one of their kind.

Example: The color I see, the sound I hear, the smells and tastes that my senses think mark the reality of things out there, are … where? Out there? But of course not! Basic science assures us that the appearance things make is not in the things themselves but in, and only in, our own experience. Is that experience determined by the things I experience, or by how the mind works?

Wait! What? I know, I know, quite astonishing. Consider the red of the red apple. Is the color not an integral possession of the apple?

That's correct! Undeniable scientific truth. There is no red in the red apple! On the surface of the apple is a reflected wavelength of light (*which is not red!*) but of just the right length that it travels up the optic nerve (so far, *no red!*) arrives at the brain's vision center and now, but not before, causes the apple to appear red.

Is it true that the red apple is red? Of course! But this is not a truth about the apple, but rather a truth about us, about how we experience the apple.

12. *Where do our ideas come from?* Perhaps we experience two different worlds, one by sense, the other by the understanding. Obvious are the ideas of sensation; neither obvious nor easy are the ideas formed by reason and applied to the world by the understanding.

Where do our ideas come from? From outside or from the operation of the mind? John Locke becomes the first anti-Cartesian Cartesian. Paradoxically, he is Cartesian, he is modern: He places the understanding of things, by way of *our own ideas*, as primary and determinative of the things we experience. However, as a staunch empiricist, he is anti-Cartesian and eschews Descartes' rationalist view of human knowledge.

No, says Locke, *reality is at the fingertip of our senses.*

John Locke. The first in the English-speaking world to fully immerse himself in, and shape his thinking to, the new Cartesian modernity. To be modern is to be certain that the proper beginning is with our own ideas. Locke's *An Essay Concerning Human Understanding* is the early English interpretation of the Cartesian insistence that philosophical concern about how-we-*know*-the-world is logically prior to (and definitive of?) a proper analysis of the *world*-that-we-know.

A high irony. Locke the Cartesian, but empiricist, turned modern by Descartes' Subjective Turn, rejects Cartesian rationalism. The ideas of a thing's qualities that Descartes so distrusts because they lack clarity and distinctness are obtained in the sense data we see, hear, touch, taste, smell, and are precisely, according to Locke's empiricism, the very mark of a thing's reality.

Whereas, according to Descartes' rationalism, sense data is so much subterfuge behind which only the understanding can find the essential nature of reality.

Keystone of Lockean empiricism: **Nothing is in the intellect that was not first in the senses** (*An Essay Concerning the Human Understanding*). Descartes' distrust of the unreliable senses motivates him to invent modern thinking. The grandest philosophical high moment: Kant's bewitching insight into the nature of knowledge. Knowledge, and the demands it makes of the world, is prior to and forms and shapes the world we come to know.

Three Awful Dogmas

1. New to philosophy and eager for a definition? Philosophy matters. Why? Look at three primal insights and taste the flavor of philosophy.

Don't miss this. The three awful dogmas of the pre-philosophical view are enforced, directed by and sanctioned by common sense.

> *Common sense is rudimentary thinking—the German for it is* **gesunder Menschenverstand**—*but it moves most easily in the medium of sense perception and imagination, and its venture beyond those limits is never whole-hearted. It feels its thought to be a thin abstraction which only borrows substance from the solid reality given in sense. Mostly it points and does not prove.*
>
> G.R.G. Mure, *An Introduction to Hegel.*

Common sense is discussed philosophically by Aristotle two-and-a-half thousand years ago. To begin biology (Aristotle's invention) it was necessary to distinguish the more elementary plants and animals from the more advanced forms of life, including mankind.

2. Aristotle notes that the plant, the most elementary life form, is defined by its basic life function to take nourishment and reproduce (the first and forever definition of life)... and biology begins.

Endowed, of course, with the life functions of plants, higher and more complex is animal life with its sensory capacities of sight and sound making possible direct and immediate intercourse with and manipulation of the world. *Enter the machine and machination of common sense.*

Between plants and man, definitive of animals, is the faculty of *aesthesis,* the physical senses of sight, sound, touch, taste and smell. But, think Aristotelians, there is everything functional but nothing exceptional about sense perception. As a basis of commerce with the physical world the senses are nothing particularly human. The empirical senses are shared by man and beast, but definitive of the beast.

3. To deploy its very *raison d'être,* common sense thinks language to be of no intrinsic vitality but only extrinsically useful as a messaging tool.

The conventional, common-sense view of language: deliver a message. We think of language as the vehicle that gathers, reports, communicates information: *The sky is falling; The wet floor is slippery; I like your hairdo.* The conventional, common-sense view of language: It is just a tool. A tool to communicate, deliver a message, and of no intrinsic importance or significance as the voice of being a person; the voice of poetry, history, and yes, of philosophy.

The Three Awful Dogmas that Infect Common Sense

[a] We are convinced that that the function, meaning, and purpose of language is *communication.* We speak to deliver a message, as do all sentient creatures. The monkey howls a warning of impending danger. Even the flower communicates, that is, interacts with its environment, by growing to the light it adores. But only man engages his world with creative thought, which has only one vehicle: language.

One example. No language, no poetry. No Robert Frost creative thought that these woods are lovely, dark, deep, and we have promises to keep, and miles to go before we sleep.

[b] *Naïve realism* is the view that the world is just as it appears to eye and ear. Can you defend your view that the world *is* just as it *looks?* Maybe the way it *looks* depends on how your *seeing works*... not on how it *is*.

[c] Truth is relative.

First Dogma: Language is for Communication

4. Language, we think, is but a device of no intrinsic value, used by all sentient creatures, as useful to man as to beast, of similar purpose to every speaker: *deliver your message.*

We think the message that rides as a passenger in the vehicle of language is significant if informational, descriptive of empirically verifiable circumstance, a report of happenstance and, because it reports what could be otherwise, informational and useful. The monkey in the overlooking tree howls a warning of incoming danger. But you and I do more in and with language than howl.

Communicators all, we model our understanding of humanness on non-human sentient behavior. Sadly, this avoids and evades the very pressing philosophical possibility that creative thought, made possible by human language, marks us as unique and separates us from the beasts. *I have promises to keep, and miles to go before I sleep* is no depiction of factual circumstance, no report of mere happenstance. The point and purpose of this speaking has nothing to do with *communication.*

What can we do in language that no elephant or monkey can do? Only you and I can ask *What is an elephant? What is a monkey?* No elephant and no monkey, but only you and I can ask *Who and what am I?* When we, in the exercise of creative thought ask *Who am I? What am I? Why am I here?* we make ourselves to *be*, we become human.

When we use language to deliver messages and when we interact with the physical world directed by common sense, we are as any other sentient creature finding our way through the day filled with challenge and opportunity.

The social sciences have taken the field, examining across all species of life the social cement of *communication* and *relationship* to tell us how we are, based on the model of the mouse and the monkey. Aha! We see the authoritarian social structure of ants and now know about the prevalence of authoritarianism in human society.

We twist our misunderstanding of language to the conceit that the world is factual, circumstantial, and happening place with language reporting what's happening. Both are very limited views of what is real and what is the revealing power of speaking.

To send a message, say how I feel, to communicate: what else, you ask, *is language for?*

There is reason, following revolutionary linguist Noam Chomsky, to believe that language brings thought alive. No thought? Then reality remains hidden, incomprehensible, un-comprehended, and unintelligible. *Thought* is not possible without *language* while much communication happens without speaking.

5. Only in language can the necessary be distinguished from happenstance, the nude from the naked, order from chaos, reality from chimera, the divine from the mundane, the significant and magnificent from the ordinary, the romantic from the classical. All this was first spoken about by the ancient Greeks as they initiated Western civilization.

Only in language can we explore the question: *What does it mean to live the good life?*

Only in language can we examine the notion: *Of all creatures, only man is capable of malicious intent.* Monkeys, men and mice all have similar physical emotional needs, but it is only man who can speak of both the divine and the evil and needs both a God and Satan.

All other creatures are innocent, formed by nature and nurture, forces outside their own deliberate choice, triggered by instinct to aggressive or defensive behavior. That is, all other creatures are restricted to and consumed by the business of common sense.

Only in language can meaning be realized:

To be or not to be ...

Any man's death diminishes me because I am involved in mankind, and therefore never send to know for whom the bell tolls; It tolls for thee ...

The unexamined life is not worth living ...

But I have promises to keep, and miles to go before I sleep ...

Today I shall be strong, No more shall yield to wrong, Shall squander life no more; Days lost, I know not how, I shall retrieve them now; Now I shall keep the vow I never kept before.

Absent language, none of the above meaningfulness is possible. This is no information to be messaged, nor is it of practical purpose. And if this is of sense, it is certainly not common, and requires the poet's and philosopher's language. None of this can occur when we are engaged in some commonsense business.

6. Review. As against the commonsense belief that the objective truth of the world is primary to, and determinative of, what we are able to think about it, there is persuasive reason to believe that the thought we construct about the world, and the very nature of the language in

which that thought is constructed, determines the world we think and speak about.

That is, some philosophers ... me, too ... think that the language in which we speak and think about the world determines the world in that way shaped and proffered, and also determines who and what we are as persons.

Think of the language of physics, of poetry, of psychology and, yes, of philosophy. Does not each language, because of their very divergent ways of constructing thought reveal different worlds?

7. Do these speak to, and about, the same world?

> *The sunbeams clasp the earth; The moonbeams kiss the sea; What are these kissings worth if thou kiss not me?*
>
> *Theirs not to reason why. Theirs but to do and die. Into the valley of death rode the six hundred.*

First a romantic, then a classical rendering of the truth of our world ... or, different worlds?

Is it the same world? By the language of physics and of common sense, seeking the classical objective truth, or by poetic speaking; is it the same world differently revealed or *are these different worlds linguistically précised?*

8. **The First Dogma of Common Sense**

All significance is descriptive, and the primary purpose of language is communication. Language is denotative, naming things and delivering messages.

But that those things are *chairs* and that other things are *tables* is just a matter of convention—objective truth cannot be found here. There is nothing *chair-like* in the word *chair*; we might as well have called them *tables* and those other things *chairs*. Life is the same so long as everyone accepts the new convention.

It is not *true* that they are chairs. The convention that we all agree to call them chairs serves, simply, to allow us to talk to one another, to communicate.

It is by arbitrary convention that vehicles on tracks are called *trains*, those airborne are called *planes*. The other way around and the world and truth would be the same.

We could just as well write on the table no matter what it was called. That I am Robert, not Richard, is a convention that aids communication, but in no way reveals any truth about me … correct?

9. Children, of course, become acquainted with the world by learning the names of things. But the time comes to rise above childish things in recognition that to know something's name is simply to adopt an arbitrary convention. Does naming it … really … talk about it?

I mean no alteration to our denoting conventions, and too, I very much hope you to fine-hone your good common sense. But let us not allow these dogmas of naïve realism to be confused as powers that reveal objective truth about human nature or apprehend necessary truth about the world.

10. Philosophers call the **Second Dogma of Common Sense** *Naïve Realism,* the commonsense view that things are—really!—just as they appear. Common sense must have it this way—else there is nothing for common sense to do, and we are a people that get things done! Absent this pre-conception (things *are* as they appear) common sense could not manipulate the practical affairs of day-in and day-out living. Again,

common sense must take for granted the unquestioned *naïve* view that the world is *real (Naïve Realism)* just as it appears.

Of course, it is not. The world appears to eye and ear not as it is, but as that appearance which is formed and shaped by how eye and ear work. Out there is no sound-that-we-hear, only vibration of air. Out there is no color, only reflection of light wave. Sound-heard and color-seen are in us, not in the world.

All our lived activity is naïve realist, practiced in the chimera of world-as-it-appears and leads to unintended consequences. Just one is the prized esteem we give to *communication* and *relationship*. These are the most overused and banal concepts but of high esteem in the common view.

To communicate is no defining characteristic of who and what we are. Everything communicates. *Relationship* is no super concept revealing the nature of us. Everything is related, in some way, to everything else. To *communicate information* and to offer factual description is no grand insight into the essential nature of things. *Relationship* is but circumstantial and no insight into the nature of us.

11. The Third ... and Most Awful ... Dogma of Common Sense: *Truth is Relative*

There are no absolutes! Call that statement x. *Is x absolute?* Well, if there are no absolutes, then, x is not absolute. That is, it is not ... it cannot be ... absolute that there are no absolutes.

The attempt to say that, *absolutely,* there are no absolutes, implodes. It is, so to speak, less than false because it has contradicted itself before it has any meaning to be true or false. In order for a statement to be true or false, it must first be meaningful ... correct? *It is absolute that there are no absolutes* is an example of a contradiction in meaning, a logical impossibility.

Let us beware self-referring statements like: *This sentence is false.* Consider: *I am firm in my opinion: all truth is opinion.* Then, logically, what you just said is not true, but rather, mere opinion, and your speaking is infirm … correct?

Again, of course, truth is not relative. That's not possible. Here's the proof. *Truth is relative* is a declarative sentence that claims, as declared by all declarative sentences, by the very nature of being a declarative sentence, to be true. *Truth is relative* makes a claim that contradicts the very being and meaning of that declaration.

But wait! *What I just said is false,* is a contradiction in terms.

12. The third dogma of common sense flows from the other two:

Words seem meaningful to the common view because they name things. Never mind that to know a thing's name brings no understanding of that thing. And let us note our tendency to think that if it has a name, then there must be something so named; a foolish commitment, don't you think? Example: the grammatically proper noun *carnivorous cow* names, well, nothing, no thing.

13. Addicted to these dogmas, common sense falls to *psychologism*, enforcing the erroneous view that truth is relative; both relative to the culture that holds its own beliefs and customs as preferable … isn't that a prejudice? … and relative to the individual who thinks that the truth of their belief is a function of their believing it.

Suffering the infection of psychologism, we think this way. *Of course, the earth is not flat, but the flat-earth view was true to medieval man.* However, that the Middle Ages were prone to false astronomical beliefs, does not make those beliefs true ... correct?

It is true that the earth is spherical. It is true today, just as true in the Middle Ages when many Europeans thought, erroneously, even though it was their common sense that the earth be flat. That someone or some culture believes some falsehood, that does not make the falsehood true ... correct? Let us give up the notion: *true to them*.

14. Common sense-isms that lead us astray:

- To know something is to know its name.
- Language is a tool; its design, purpose and significance is to communicate.
- The world is—really!—just as it appears.
- Truth is (culturally and individually) relative.

Philosophy is Not Difficult ... We Are!

1. My favorite philosopher, eighteenth-century Irishman, George Berkeley: *First we have raised a cloud of dust and then we complain we cannot see* (*Treatise, Introduction*).

In the early twentieth century, Cambridge analytic philosopher Ludwig Wittgenstein (student, then colleague of Bertrand Russell) likened the perplexity of philosophers to buzzing flies caught in a bottle. All we need do is uncork the bottle of absurdity and confusion that pervades conventional speaking and let them (the philosophy flies) out into the clarity of sound reasoning and clear thinking.

What prevents sound reasoning and clear thinking? Knots of perplexity are not in philosophy, but in our postmodern commitment to ... wait for it ... *common sense*.

> *We all start from naïve realism, i.e., the doctrine that things are what they seem. We think that grass is green, that stones are hard and that snow is cold. But physics assures us that the greenness of the grass, the hardness of stones and the coldness of the snow are not the greenness, hardness and coldness that we know in our own experience, but something very different. The observer, when he seems to himself to be*

observing a stone, is really, if physics is to be believed, observing the effect of the stone upon himself. Naïve realism ... is false.

> Bertrand Russell, *Inquiry into Meaning and Truth.*

The person who has no tincture of philosophy goes through life imprisoned in the prejudices derived from common sense, from the habitual beliefs of his age or his nation, and from convictions which have grown up in his mind without the cooperation or consent of his deliberate reason.

> Bertrand Russell, "The Value of Philosophy," *The Problems of Philosophy.*

Common sense is rudimentary thinking—the German for it is **gesunder menschen verstand**—*but it moves most easily in the medium of sense perception and imagination, and its venture beyond those limits is never whole-hearted. It feels its thought to be a thin abstraction which only borrows substance from the solid reality given in sense. Mostly it points and does not prove.*

> G.R.G. Mure, *An Introduction to Hegel.*

Universally prized and admired, common sense is recommended to those thought to be on a wayward path. Parents eagerly instruct children. We are certain that sophisticated common sense is necessary, perhaps even sufficient, to gain a successful life plan and is at least a pre-requisite to a life lived well.

But listen to Thomas Paine: *The World is my country, all mankind are my brethren, and to do good is my religion.* Paine called his earth-shaking pamphlet *Common Sense*, but here there is nothing common and Paine's *sense* is in the sense of sensibility, *intelligibility.*

2. Exercising practical skills, fine-honed by habit, common sense tackles the demands of physical circumstance. We train our children to well handle challenges and opportunities for social and financial success. We think this the highest life purpose or, at least, the pre-requisite for a life lived well.

Common sense: *Look left, look right, then left again before you step off the curb. Know when to hold 'em and when to fold 'em.* For survival's sake, be aware of the probable consequence, then choose flight or fight.

Again, let's be aware that there is nothing *common* in Thomas Paine's *Common Sense*. But this firebrand pamphlet lit the firecracker of liberty in both eighteenth-century revolutionary America and France. I wish Paine had not called it that.

These are the times that try men's souls. And the rag-tag colonial Americans went to revolution against the strongest military power in the world. That's not common sensical.

Philosophy cannot happen in, but is a reflection on the ordinary and mundane. Philosophy is a reflection on the difference between common sense and sensibility. That darned ambiguity: not the senses by eye and ear but sensibility in the sense of intelligibility. Philosophy knows it can only take place as we suspend and transcend common and casual concerns, including the concerns and goals of common sense. Philosophy and common sense: like oil and water.

3. Common sense is discussed by Aristotle two-and-a-half thousand years ago. To begin biology (yes, biology is Aristotle's invention) it is necessary to distinguish the more elementary plants and animals from the more advanced forms of life, including mankind.

Aristotle says that the plant, the most elementary life form, is defined by its basic life function to take nourishment and reproduce. This is the first and forever definition of life. Higher and more complex is animal life endowed, of course, with the life functions of plants, but more, with the senses of sight and sound to make possible direct and immediate intercourse with the world. That is, with the sensory facilities that empower common sense.

All sentient creatures not only take nourishment and reproduce but, to assure successful intercourse with their environment, smoothly *communicate* and form efficacious *relationships*. Common sense knows that language has this purpose! To deliver messages! Speech is for communication! Persuasive rhetoric is the oldest academic discipline in the history of the western world and must be fine honed to guarantee advantageous *relationships*.

Listen to the social sciences of psychology, sociology and anthropology: *Communication* and *relationship* are the social cement needed to achieve a life lived well. Poetry and philosophy are, well, frills, perhaps silly, but certainly not consequential to common sense.

Enter the work and goal of common sense. All sentient creatures, man and beast alike, interacting with their immediate environs, goal to practical purpose, operate within the physical realm of fact, of information, of the physically practically possible. To do its work, common sense cannot be bothered with what is necessarily the case. What *must* be and *cannot* change is irrelevant to the practical purposes of common sense.

Irrelevant? What cannot be other than it happens to be is but an obstacle to, and irrelevant to, the practical business of molding circumstances and states of affairs to our common-sensical purpose. Common sense manipulates, well, what can be manipulated. Common sense has no interest in either what must be the case or what cannot be manipulated.

4. Special to animals is the faculty of *aesthesis* (the Greek root for our *aesthetic*)—the physical senses of sight and sound, touch, taste, and

smell. But, think Aristotelians, there is everything functional but nothing exceptional about sense perception as a basis of commerce with the physical world. The senses are nothing particularly human, but, of course, the senses are the medium in which operates the good practical common sense—operated by man and beast alike.

Common sense, and all its operation, is limited to the realm of information, the factual, the practical, the possible. Common sense, stuck in the realm of physical existence, insists that values, including ethics and aesthetics, are but sentiment and have no objective reality.

Listen to commonsense philosopher, A.J. Ayer:

> ...*[S]tatements of value...are not in the literal sense significant, but they are simply expressions of emotion which can be neither true nor false. The exhortation to moral virtue are not propositions at all, but ejaculations or commands.*
>
> A Critique of Ethics.

The empirical senses specialize in the appearance of things, in happenstance, factual description of what happens to be the case. Successful interaction with the experienced world, organized and driven by common sense, is shared by man and beast, but definitive of the beast. Definitive of man: *the search for the objective truth of virtue and value, the divine, the excellent and the exquisite.*

5. This is how we (mis)understand the human condition. We think the work of the senses, including common sense, is the purpose of life. We see ourselves as subjective entities *out-side* the objective world. Subjectively, we reach into the world's objective physical existence to manipulate what we find to our own purposes. This is the conventional pre-philosophical attitude about life, about our location vis-a-vis the experienced world as confirmed by common sense.

To do its work of describing how the world behaves, natural science, the social sciences, and too, common sense, must assume the things that co-habit our world are independent of us, are constituted prior to our arrival, and unaffected—certainly not determined—by our sensible awareness and our understanding of things.

We think that objective reality remains obstinately unchanged and impervious to our empirical discovery of it. Science, and pre-philosophical common sense, assume that the reality of the experienced world persists unchanged, whether we know about it or not.

Contemporary philosophy disagrees and investigates the view that *how* we see determines *what* we see, and *how* we know determines *what* we know, especially as philosophy is practiced in France and Germany.

6. I think we spend too much of our life and too much of our time running after the ordinary demands of day-in and day-out living, directed by common sense. Listen to Bertrand Russell (in *In Praise of Idleness*):

> *I think that there is too much work done in the world, that immense harm is caused by the belief that work is virtuous.*

Russell goes on to explain that a wise use of leisure is needed for a life lived well, lived as a self-determining person.

> *The wise use of leisure ... is a product of education and civilization ... it (leisure) contributed nearly the whole of what we call civilization. It cultivated the arts and discovered the sciences; it wrote the books, invented the philosophies, and defined social relations ... Without the leisure class, mankind would never have emerged from barbarism.*

Commonly, life is lived in the world of *doxa. Doxa,* as the Greeks would say, *what appears, what seems* by sense experience and self-serving commonsense opinion to pursue practical affairs and deal with our physical needs and desires.

From childhood on, we live to find out what we (are supposed to) like and value. Then we elevate what we like to be *true*. By common sense, *truth* is a practical business and becomes what works in this time and place, as convenient to and made available by *my* group, my gang, all of us conforming to the diktat of the commune.

7. What defines man and distinguishes him from all other life, including the other sentient creatures capable of sight and sound, is not the common sense that all sentient creatures including man, must exercise in order to get on, but *man's rational ability to know objective truth, the essential nature of reality, what is necessary about things*. No other creature, only man, strives to appreciate the lovely, the exquisite, the divine. When man accomplishes that, he accomplishes himself.

My view is that the purpose of philosophy is achieved with an appreciation of this insight.

My argument is that common sense is the best the beast has to come to terms with its world. Man has not only common sense, but with the more divine faculties of reason and understanding does man find both the essential reality of his world, and of himself.

That makes man the only creature responsible to create himself and, too, to be the appreciator of the world, a world that remains silent and dark until man brings essential reality to light and to his enlightenment.

8. **The Trouble with Common Sense**

Not philosophy, but *we* are difficult. Our difficulty: Imprisoned by the senses—especially common sense—to the challenges of ever-changing existence, and with our faculties shackled to the physical world of appearance and random circumstance, we are not free to dream the dreams of philosophy.

What dreams? Listen to Bertrand Russell's dream:

Is there any knowledge in the world which is so certain that no reasonable man could doubt it?

"Appearance and Reality" in *Problems of Knowledge.*

Certain about what? About the objective, undeniable truth—not just a description—of who and what we are. And the undeniable truth—not just a description—of the meaning of the world, and our place and relation to it.

9. For the narrow width of its deliberations and decisions, and the shallow depth of its conclusions, common sense sees only and works only on physicality, on factual information gathered by the physical senses. The mark and measure of its concerns: what is sensibly received by eye and ear! Its purpose: ease the path to achieve practical goals. Common sense will have no truck with anything that feeds the imagination, requires creative thought, educated discernment or any of the finer things of human life.

I want to say again: *In order to do their work, science, technology, and pre-philosophical common sense assume the priority of physical things out there that then invites science and common sense to do their manipulations.* It seems intuitively unavoidable, the logical conclusion seems inexorable: *We come to know about things because, first, there are things to know about which precede our experience and present themselves for our encounter with them. Situations and circumstance must first be present for common sense to seek manipulative advantage.*

10. The First Dogma of Common Sense: Language is for Communication, the Vehicle That Delivers Messages.

Common sense prizes *communication* and, too, *relationship*. These are the most overused and banal concepts but of high esteem in both the common view and the descriptive social sciences. Physicalist common sense sees the purpose and value of language: *communication*, the simple delivery of message and the naming of things that occupy our experience of the world. As though, if you know its name, you therefore know what it is.

But, everything communicates. The flower communicates with the light it needs by growing toward a light source. The spring water communicates with its stream bed by running faster or slower depending on incline.

Everything has some relationship to everything else. Everything is of some spatial and temporal distance from everything else. The list of *relationships* goes on.

Here, on the humanities side of investigation, we insist that to know about A and/or B, more is needed than description of how they look and how they work and how they are *related*.

Listen to linguist Noam Chomsky in a casual *You Tube* conversation:

> *There are a number of dogmas about language ... that language is primarily a means of communication, and that it evolved as a means of communication. Probably that's totally false. It seems that language evolved and is designed as a mode of creating and interpreting thought. It can be used to communicate; everything people do can be used to communicate. You communicate by your hair style, style of walk.*

> *And, yes, language can be used to communicate, but it doesn't seem to be part of its design. Its design seems to be radically different; and it (its design) seems to undermine communication. If you look carefully, case after case, you find that right at the core of its design, where there are conflicts between what would be efficient for communication and what would be efficient for specific biological design of language and in every case that is known ... efficiency for communication is sacrificed.*

Language and Thought, You Tube.

11. *Naïve Realism*, the Second Dogma of Common Sense

Naive Realism: *All things are—really!—just as they appear. All significance is descriptive and a primary purpose of communicative language is denotational.* The senses gather impressions, and this sense data of appearance indisputably represents truth. This oh-so-pervasive, from childhood on, naïve realist view thinks our subjective impressions report objective reality. To *know* requires only to name the things we see, and hear, touch, taste and smell.

But there is nothing *chair-like* in the word *chair;* we might as well have called them, say, *tables* (and those other things *chairs*). Life would be the same so long as everyone followed the new convention.

Children, of course, become acquainted with the world by learning the names of things. But familiarity bred by awareness of things should not be confused with conscious apprehension of what they mean and what makes them to be real. The time comes to put aside childish things, transcend awareness, achieve understanding. Example: recognize that to know something's name is simply to adopt an arbitrary convention.

The correct insight: to *talk about it* is the only way to intelligibly *think about it*. But does naming it really talk about it?

12. The Third—and Most Devastating—Dogma of Common Sense: *Truth is Relative*

There are no absolutes! Call that statement *x*. Is *x* absolute? Well, if there are no absolutes, then, *x* is not absolute. That is, it is not *absolute* that there are no absolutes.

The attempt to say that *absolutely* there are no absolutes implodes. It is less than false because it has contradicted itself before there is any meaning to be true or false. For a statement to be true or false, it must first be meaningful... correct? *It is absolute that there are no absolutes* is an example of a contradiction in meaning and a logical impossibility.

Allan Bloom tells us, in *Closing of the American Mind*, that incoming students in his University of Chicago courses are certain there is no certainty.

Call *There are no truths* statement x. Is x true? Well, if there are no truths, then statement x is not true. That is, it is not true that there are no truths. The attempt at the relativity of truth implodes; *There are no truths,* contradicts itself.

To assert is inherently a claim of truth. A proclamation against its own intention is self-defeating, like saying *This statement is false*, which means the same as *This statement contradicts itself.* The speech act, or act of thinking, that so-and-so is such-and-such cannot be separated from the intention that what is said is asserted because it is true.

Beware of self-referring statements like *This statement is false* or *This statement is relatively-true depending on who is saying it.* If it is true that all truths are relative, then the *offered-as-true-statement* that all *truths are relative* is itself relative and, therefore, not true.

I am firm in my opinion: All supposed truth is opinion. Then, logically, what you just said is not true, but infirm opinion...correct?

13. In this postmodern era, our classical edge, God help us, brings us to depend upon gadgets and technology. Our romantic edge brings us to retreat to *psychologism*. Postmodernism thinks that truth, value, virtue, ethics, beauty, excellence are, well, emotions. These are not substantive and objective, to be understood as metrics of the meaning of life, but psychological states to be felt, lived in, experienced.

Marshall McLuhan's grand insight into postmodernism: old-fashioned *square* people are content-oriented; contemporary *cool* people do not encounter, analyze, and explain the world, but rather explore how it *feels*.

This is a move away from the traditional West that wants to understand, and for millennia, put our experience of the world to a scientific and philosophic analysis. This is a postmodern wink at the East that thinks the world is *authentically* (what does that even mean?) available to us only through our active participation in it—with it—and immediately.

How romantic! Only intimacy and commitment count. As T.S. Eliot says in *Love Song of J. Alfred Prufrock:* **Do not ask what is it; let us make our visit.**

14. *Psychologism* is the view that the truth of assertions, and too, valid inference, are mental events and personal psychological possessions. *Psychologism* egocentrically renders subjective what is objectively independent of what and how we know. *Psychologism* makes truth and value relative to and based on the person or the culture that so believes.

In today's postmodernism, our classical edge, a retreat of all else to subjective psychologism: if you think it, like it, then believe it. Truth, value, ethics, virtue, beauty, excellence are but subjective states to be lived in. Emotions are not objective truths to be understood; not truths that reveal the essential nature of things that occupy our experience of the world.

Why do incoming university students think that truth is—must be—relative, and of no objective substance? Common sense falls to psychologism, the view that truth is relative to the culture that holds its own customs and beliefs as preferable and relative to the individual who thinks that the truth of their beliefs is a function of their believing it.

In the common parlance of common sense: Of course the Earth is not flat, but the flat-Earth view was *true* to medieval man. However, that the Middle Ages were prone to false astronomical beliefs does not make those false beliefs true... correct?

15. Curious. Language is user dependent. No speaker, no thinker, then no meaning is thought or spoken. Too much focus here could lower this notion to a truism. One may then be tempted to psychologism: the error of signifying truth and significance to be a function of someone's awareness of truth and significance. As though $2 + 2 = 4$ is not true if no one knows about it, and true only when someone thinks it.

We, vessels of truth and significance, so thoroughly subjective instruments we are. But it takes a speaker, a thinker, to bring truth and significance, so to speak, alive, or, at least to conscious awareness and attention. Only you and I can do this. All creatures communicate, build relationship one to another based on delivering and receiving messages. Only you and I, in language, do more than communicate messages and form relationships.

Truth and significance remain quiet, hidden beneath the intrusive, vivacious appearance of things, waiting for a speaker. Does that place a special obligation on us?

Can Philosophy Change Your Life?

Part I

1. We are so confident in our taken for granted, undefended and indefensible certainties which shape our world view.

Some philosophical reflection could change your understanding of yourself and your world. I very much hope you will consider this life changing philosophical view. This view requires an open-minded willingness to question favorite and most entrenched common-sense shibboleths.

2. You know what you are thinking, feeling, imagining. You can be confident in your own impressions and ideas. No one and nothing can fool you about that. But can you be certain about anything beyond your own ideas? Example. Can you defend your view that your subjective experience is an accurate report caused by an objective world *out there*?

Whew! What? Wait! No *out-there* out there? *Gosh!* This is the first time you have been asked to question the foundation and the source of immediate and direct sensory experience. I know, I know: *Ask me about anything, but not that!* Seems too outlandish to consider. No *out-there* out there? Day-in and day-out business would be flummoxed.

3. Begin here. *Out there? Where is that?* I think we will agree you cannot be mistaken that you are thinking this or that thought and you cannot be mistaken that you are aware of what appears, let's say, green. But you believe the green apple you are holding in your hand and biting into exists outside your experience. You think it causes your experience. Thinking like this is easy on our intuitive sense of things, convenient ... but unwarranted. Pugnacious philosophy demands: *prove it!*

Here's the common, ordinary view of which we are so certain. We think the world, together with all the things that occupy our experience of the world, is objective, previous and prior to our encounter with them. We think things remain unaffected whether or not we see them or know about them. So entrenched in the common understanding is this taken for granted view.

Objective is the world prior to, separate from, cause of and source for our *subjective* experience. Our intuition would not have it any other way. We think these objective and subjective realms to be stand-alones, independent of and non-determinative of each other. We think the out-there realm precedes and is the primary source for our subjective conscious experience.

But there is philosophical reason to believe it is just the other way around. This astonishing notion and grandest insight of contemporary philosophy: Perhaps *how* we know determines *what* we know. Perhaps what we know is limited to what is knowable about the things that occupy our experience of the world. *Knowable about things?* As determined by ... what? By the structure of the understanding that demands things that occupy our experience of the world present themselves in just such a way that we can know them.

4. I mean to demonstrate that *how* you understand the world *determines* your world and *how* you understand yourself *determines* who and what you are. Certainty is restricted to our own ideas, to the realm of

self-reflection, to only that which occupies consciousness. There is reason to be skeptical about all that seems to be out there, outside consciousness.

We are certain that seven plus five equals twelve and that a straight line is the shortest distance between two points. Intelligibility demands that these are, well, certainly true. Can we be certain, or should we be skeptical about what is reported by eye and ear? I think we should be skeptical. Here's why.

5. Everyone will agree: Our only immediate and direct access to the world is through the senses of seeing, touching, hearing, smelling, and tasting. These cannot help but gather in the flood of physical characteristics that pour out of the appearance existing things make to eye and ear.

Let's look at what the senses receive. Well, obviously, not the thing we are sure is out there, but that thing's appearance. If it exists, we can see it; If we can perceive it, it exists ... correct? We see the red of the red apple; hear, taste and smell the crunch of our bite. And we are, of course, certain about these impressions and sensations.

Any certainty that they are caused by an apple out there?

Where are all these physical characteristics gathered in by eye and ear? The undeniable truth that shocks common sense: not *in* the apple, but *in*, and only *in*, our own seeing and tasting the apple. I know, I know: This undeniable truth is so counter-intuitive. *What!? No red in the red apple!?*

Certainly correct, if basic science is to be believed. There is no *red* in the red apple! Basic science assures us that in (better, *on*) the apple's surface is a reflected wavelength of light (no light, no color) *which is itself not red,* and which enters the eye, travels the optic nerve (so far, no red!) and excites the vision center of the brain. Now, and only now, is there the experience of red.

This is not a philosophic conjecture but undeniable basic science. The above scientific note about red applies equally to all other physical characteristics of the crunch as we bite into the apple; too, of the sound we hear, the scent we smell.

6. We think—and we are so certain—that the apple is *real* because it *exists*. But, as seen above, every mark of existence, every physical characteristic, is not *in* the apple, but *in*, and *only* in, our own experience of the apple.

You believe that its existence marks its reality. You think its existence *means* it is real; Its reality *means* it exists. But... wait... please... you do not, you cannot, experience *existence*. You only experience bits of appearance, red and the other physical characteristics in a biting crunch, all of which are in you.

I know, I know. So anti-intuitive. I so hope you consider that things are, of course, real, but not real because they exist. I know you will agree: The green of the green apple is no mark of the apple's reality.

A nice question: What makes the apple to be real? That it is red, round, ripe? What about rotten green ones? Again, what is inherently and intrinsically *in* the apple that makes it to be real?

Again, none of the crunch is *in* the apple, it is *in* us. Philosophical reflection begins here. If, as demonstrated above, none of the crunch is *in* the apple, but *in* us, *what is in the apple?* There must be something *in* the apple; after all the apple is *real*. What makes it to be *real?*

Part II

7. This is not an essay on apples, but an investigation into the nature of value. I argue that value, and only this, is inherent and intrinsic within the apple. Its value is its essential nature. If you will, its *apple-ness*.

How real is anything that occupies our experience of the world? More than two thousand years ago, Plato and his student, Aristotle, argued that how *good* (Plato) is a thing, (Aristotle) how well achieved and accomplished it is: That's the metric of how real it is. Notice, I did not ask the more usual question: Is it real? From Plato and Aristotle, a nice philosophical insight: Reality is not, as we tend to think, an *is* or *is not* determination, but a matter of degree. That is, ancient Greek philosophy understands that a better one is more real.

That's it! Don't you see? The red of the red apple, and all the other physical characteristics contained in the of appearance it makes, floods our physical senses. Red and crunchy and all we see and feel, smell, touch and taste are *in* us. What then is *in* the apple? What but *apple-ness*.

It is difficult to deny Plato's view that *The Good* as the very measure of reality is, therefore, more real than any good thing it reveals. It is difficult to refute Aristotle's argument that real is a thing's virtue. The astonishing new way to understand our world: The value of things—not the simple brute fact(s) of their existence makes them to be real.

Hidden from eye and ear, hidden under its deceptive veil of appearance, lying dormant and waiting for you to intend it and educate your empirical experience of it, is its essential nature. That is, this measures the apple: how well it exemplifies what it means for anything to be an apple.

8. Consider a straight-backed, four-legged, plain wooden chair. That it is brown: does that make it to be real? That it is four-legged? Are not rockers real chairs? That it is made of wood? Are not metal chairs real? Isn't it correct that all these physical characteristics cannot be gathered

together to mark and measure its reality as a chair? All these physical characteristics gather together to mark and measure the non-essential idiosyncrasies and accidental characteristics of this particular chair ... correct?

Now, this mental experiment. Cut off one-half inch from the bottom of one of its four legs. Doesn't sit quite as well as it used to ... correct? Undeniable it is not quite as good a chair as it used to be. Continue to break away a piece here and there until, viola, no more chair, just a pile of wooden scraps.

Somewhere along the process of molesting the chair by breaking away a part here and there, it was becoming less good (as a chair) until, finally, it stopped being a chair. And, now, just a pile of debris.

Just when? Don't know. But I know this. Each small piece broken away from the chair made it less good a chair ... correct? How do I know? Just sit in it and you will *see*. Pardon the pun.

9. What then is *in* the chair that marks and measures its reality? What but how good a chair it is; its value.

Part III

10. Can philosophy change your life? Philosophy offers alternatives to the childish, vulgar, ordinary, naïve realist view that the world is objectively and simply somehow somewhere out there. We tend to think the world is outside consciousness primping its appearance to suit your senses, waiting for you to notice it.

How you understand both the world and yourself will determine both the world you choose and the you that chooses it. Choose? How? Philosophically.

Certainty

1. Pussycats are elegant, but they don't know it. Elephants are ponderous, monkeys are nimble, but they don't know it. You do. Elegance, ponderosity, nimbleness are essential about them. Let us distinguish what is essential and certain from what is possible but not necessary. Knowing what is certain and essential about things is essential about you.

An inelegant pussycat? A non-ponderous elephant? As impossible as a carnivorous cow.

Not only is it the case that you and I, and no other creature, can know this but we know it with the only vehicle that can make knowledge possible, *language*.

In no other way can essential truth be apprehended. In no vehicle other than language can the distinction be made between that which is certain (*pussycats are elegant, monkeys are nimble and agile*) and that which is possible or probable. Only you and I can know such things. Only persons can distinguish between the essential and the circumstantial.

Only you and I can distinguish the essentialness of things, what is certainly true about them (*wish we had a word for such formidable knowledge*) from circumstantial description, from random happenstance.

2. Too young or too naïve, you may not yet know it is certain that cats are elegant or what it means to say that elephants are ponderous

and monkey agility is admirable and adorable. Perhaps you are not yet versed in matters of logic and value. We will wait for you to grow up, become a person, and value *virtue*, the necessary truth of things.

Necessarily true! I like certainties that illuminate and reveal the inherent reality of things: The *virtue* of a cat is its inherent elegance; The *virtue* of a monkey is its nimble agility. Elegance and agility define the things that possess them and reveal what it means to be one of those things.

3. It is important to note that virtue is not available to eye and ear but to the understanding. No other creature, including human children, know such things. Only a person endowed with reality-intending understanding can distinguish between what happens to be the case, *information*, and what is certain, necessary and must be true.

Much of what we think we know is happenstance, non-essential and descriptive of random occurrence. That's the definition of *information*, available to eye and ear. To gather information is a faculty common to man and beast. But pussycats do not know they are elegant. That's a higher sort of knowledge—knowledge of essential reality—that requires understanding, and is exclusive to mankind, and the gods.

We really should have a name for knowledge intended by the understanding that reveals the essentialness of things. We really should have a name for knowledge of the inherent reality if things.

4. Oh! These so empirical times! It surprises me that we prize information over certainty. Information is available to man and beast alike. But only you and I, no other creature, can distinguish between happenstance and certainty. In the practical course of life, we are inundated with contingency, and so we ignore necessity. We are doers. There is nothing to be done about what is necessary and cannot be changed. Nor have we any reason to.

But it does not satisfy if knowledge of the world is limited to the casual. As to the things that occupy our experience of the world, I want to know what is *certainly* true. Simple description does not satisfy my desire to know my world, and to know myself.

If I do not know what it means: *pussycats are elegant*, then all I know about cats is just record keeping. Correct?

5. Review. What we get by eye and ear is informational, descriptive, factual. What cannot be otherwise is not information. Necessary truth is a bother and an obstacle to the common sense business of day-in and day-out practical life. Information fuels the fire of common sense.

What must be the case is not confirmed by eye but by logic and meaning. This is to know as only a person can. I say: Let me know the meaning of things, their value, their virtue, their what-it-means-to-be-one-of-their-kind. Whew! That says a lot, might be quite anti-intuitive, should be read again, slowly.

6. Let us notice the different vectors. Information from appearances floods the senses, *from* the appearance of things *to* eye and ear. But to do its work, the understanding must reach for, find and grasp essential and necessary truth. Uniquely human understanding intends and then apprehends the essential reality that lays hidden behind the appearance of an ever-shifting world.

If and when we do, only then is essential reality revealed. If and when we do, only then do we become persons.

Is that what it means to have a soul?

Again, it is certain—necessarily true—that pussycats are graceful and elegant, cumbersome elephants are ponderous, monkeys, agile and nimble. This is not mere factual information but knowledge certain, revealing the intrinsic and inherent and necessary knowledge of what makes pussycats and elephants and monkeys real.

7. In common and ordinary speaking and thinking, *certainty* is a *disposition*, about *us*, not about the things that occupy our experience of the world. I am *certain* that my watch and keys will be in the same place I put them last night. It is, of course, possible that this will not be the case, even though I am so sure.

There is a very real sense in which descriptive facts, *that's redundant*, confirmed by empirical experience are as subjective as imaginations, preferences, and opinions. The ancient Greeks who initiated philosophy and Western civilization, knew to be skeptical of the significance of facts and lumped them together with feelings under the label, *doxa*. *Doxa*: all together, feelings and facts, ideas and impressions determined —not by objective reality, but—by our own inner, subjective operation of the sensibility.

The Greeks regarded empirical information, detected by eye and ear, and of no necessity, to be of the same ilk as imaginings, feelings, personal idiosyncrasies.

Not us. We tend to value the possible because it is informative. We tend to be unimpressed with necessity because what must be the case cannot be changed and is of no practical significance. And we are a practical people who get things done.

8. What must be the case, like *all men are mortal* or *all bachelors are unmarried*, are logically necessary but say nothing significant. Speak about *men* and, of course, you are speaking about *mortal* beings. Talk about *bachelors* and, of course, you are talking about *men unwed*.

9. It looks like an unhappy choice. It seems that speaking, and thinking, of things is either informative and interesting, but unessential and not certain, or, certain, but un-informative and un-interesting.

Here is what we want and need, as persons responsible for the world we experience: *knowledge that is both informative and necessarily true.*

10. This is the knowledge I want: necessary *and informative.* It is not happenstance that felines are elegant. They *must* be. Elegance is necessarily and certainly true of pussycats. Too, elegance is an essential ingredient of their very being. It is not possible to be a pussycat and not elegant.

I believe this is the grandest accomplishment in all the history of philosophy: Immanuel Kant's discovery and explanation for knowledge both *necessary* and *significant.* Let's sidestep the jargon and go at once to Kantian examples.

Seven plus five equals twelve. A straight line is the shortest distance between two points.

11. *Informative* necessities? Here's why. A child doing their numbers may well understand what it means to add together and find the sum of two numbers. The child may know what it means to add five to seven, but not yet know that twelve is the result.

A *straight line* is a matter of quality; *shortest distance* is a matter of quantity. The meaning of one is not contained in nor inferred by the other. *A straight line is the shortest distance between two pints*: necessarily true, and, too, significant.

The meaning of *unwed* is already part of and required by the meaning of *bachelor*; nothing new to be gleaned from *bachelors are unwed.* The meaning of *mortal* is already part of and required by the meaning of *men*; nothing new to be gleaned from *men are mortal*.

Bachelors are unwed, and *all men are mortal.* These certainties are simply analytic and in no sense about the world. These certainties are about, and only about the meaning of the words: *men, mortal, bachelor, unwed. Seven plus five equals twelve* and *A straight line is the shortest distance between two points* are examples of the kind of knowledge I want. By God, I want to know what is certainly true, but also significant about the world.

I admire insights into the certain essentialness of things, like *pussycats are elegant, elephants are ponderous, monkeys are nimble.*

Is there any certainty about the things that occupy our experience of the world? Yes! Plato wants us to judge how *good* they are. Aristotle wants to know their *virtue*, how well accomplished and achieved they are as measured by what they are meant to be, as measured by what they mean, and not just how they happen to look.

12. Review. If a child, or other sort of innocent knows only how things look, and this certainty, that *pussycats are elegant* is explained to them, then they have taken an important first step into becoming philosophically sophisticated. Namely, they are introduced to the *for-persons-only* distinction between what is accidental, factually descriptive, versus what is certain, necessarily true, *and informative.*

Now you are ready for philosophy. Now you realize how tantalizing and significant is the question: *Is there any certainty concerning the things that occupy my experiences of the world? Or is all knowledge information, factual, haphazard, random happenstance? Is knowledge restricted to the appearance things make to eye and ear? Is my world just a random flux of flotsam and jetsam pulled hither and dither by the tides of chance? Is there no certainty in my knowledge of the world?*

13. The ordinary, conventional, pervasive, physicalist view (about our world) is *empiricist (all we know is from the senses)*. When we think *cat*, we think four-legged, furry, less than thirty pounds. This is a mistake, not because some of us are dog people, but because of the physicalist, empiricist prejudice that delimits our encounter with our world to its appearance.

Restrict our experience of the world to factual description, mistaking information as the mark and measure of the real. That relegates the essential that cannot be detected by eye or ear to the dustbin of analytic, uninformative necessity.

You may need an education to find out about elegance and other values and virtues, and their central role in revealing the reality of things. Until you discover the necessary truth of it, you may not be certain about the essentialness of elegance to felineness. But it is certain that the notion of an inelegant cat is an anomaly.

So, let us distinguish between inconsequential physical description and our uniquely human facility to grasp essential truth. At stake: Which world do you choose to live in? Do you choose the easy world of random circumstance, or the world of essential and necessary truth that requires you to rev up the pro-active intentionality of the understanding?

14. Listen to Bertrand Russell in what is called the best introduction to philosophy in the English language.

> **IS there any knowledge in the world which is so certain that no reasonable man could doubt it? This question, which at first sight might not seem difficult, is really one of the most difficult that can be asked ...**

In the search for certainty, it is natural to begin with our present experiences, and in some sense, no doubt, knowledge is to be derived from them. But any statement as to what it is that our immediate experiences make us know is very likely to be wrong.

"Appearance and Reality" in *Problems of Knowledge.*

We need to explore this exciting possibility. Is there, and are we capable of apprehending, information about our world that not only informs but also is certain? Are we capable of knowledge both informative and essential, necessarily true, significant and certain and consequential? The successful search for significant certainty is our grandest intellectual achievement and marks the initiation of contemporary philosophy by the German thinker, Immanuel Kant, over two centuries ago.

Words

1. Some words are lovely. They taste good and sound deliciously.

Words: how they taste and sound, a romantic notion. On the other hand, classically, words are the repository and structure and vehicle of truth—what work they do!

Classically and logically, words are where truth lives! Aristotle's first work—even before his *First Philosophy* (The *Metaphysics*) came The *Organon* (usually translated as *The Instrument of Truth*). I prefer *Truth-Engine*.

Aristotle taught the Western world that truth is of a logical structure. We bring truth to light by selecting something to talk about (the subject), then saying something relevant and revealing about it (the predicate).

All men (the subject) are (the predicate) *mortal.* True! *The cat is on the mat; The water is wet; Mars is bigger than Mercury.* Truth as a construction of subject/predicate assertion declares that so-and-so is such-and-such. That's logic. That's classical. That's the classical, logical structure of truth, first formulated by Aristotle more than two millennia ago in his, now our, correspondence *Theory of Truth.*

2. In ordinary speaking, *truth* is ambiguous. By *true Englishman born*, Shakespeare means as English as English-can-be: *true love*, a *true patriot*,

truly yours (these are not about truth but sincerity) a carpenter's *true line*, called *plumb*, absolutely vertical or horizontal.

None of these have anything to do with philosophical truth, that is, primal *truth*, the denial of which is *false*.

Ain't that the truth! A cute and confused notion of truth that is simply another piece of ordinary language veering away from the logical notion of truth. *Ain't that the truth!* is not about truth but is an expression of admiration, a way to emphasize that we like and agree with what was just said.

3. By *truth* I mean the primal, philosophical, logical notion of truth. I mean that which is opposed to what is false. Let's note that *falsely yours* (What could that mean?) is no denial of *truly yours*. *False English born* has no meaning at all. A *love that is true* has nothing to do with truth but with commitment and sincerity.

Philosophy of language is interested in understanding the structure of meaning that then can be said to be true and not false. Yes, words bring truth, but it is not the physical occurrence of words that is true, but their meaning—what philosophers call the *proposition*. If it is true that *it is raining,* then, it is true that *esta lloviendo* (Spanish words) and it is true that *es regnet* (German words). *Words* are not true, true or false are the meanings that words bring to light.

The Latin lilt does not make Spanish words true; the guttural Germanic does not make German words true. That it is actually, in fact, *raining* makes those words convey truth. Not the physical occurrence of the language but the meaning carried by language—not the words, but the meanings of the words, are—must be—propositionally true or false.

What makes propositional meaning true? When the propositional structure of language corresponds to the structure of reality ... aha! Truth.

4. A nice philosophical insight here: The keystone to reality are not things but idealities, not words, but meanings. Truth does not lie in the physical occurrence of words but in the *meanings* they carry. That Dimitri says it in Russian or Gertrude writes it in German or Luis thinks it in Spanish, does not make the physical occurrence of what is thought to be true or false. True (or false) are not words but the *meaning* brought by words.

This raises a nice philosophical question: Where are those meanings? The truth of things is not itself a thing and not out-there alongside the things about which words speak. And we will notice, if there is a world of things out-there, they are—at least as far as they appear to the senses—poor limited things, blemished by the rigors of existence, matters of happenstance. None of this can be said about propositional, meaningful truth.

Truth is not a function of authorship. *True to them* is neither true nor false but merely opinion. True are *propositions*: the meaning of assertions that accurately assess the world. True are *propositions*: Propositions are the meaning of assertions. *Propositional truth:* The truth of declarations that so-and-so is, truly, such-and-such. Truth in language is engendered by subject/predicate assertion. Again, so-and-so is such-and-such.

Let us notice that *apple* is not true; *red* is not true; but we can construct truth in the subject/predicate form, *The apple is red*. Thank you, Aristotle: truth is materially circumstantial, true by accurate apprehension of *what is*. But not true because we apprehend it. But it needs to be noted, if we do not apprehend it, where and when would truth be?

To assert the objective truth of things is to know about the world, and to know our proper location in the world, i.e., as knowers of the world—only you and I can do that. All sentient creatures, including you and I, are aware of circumstantial happenstance, but only you and I can distinguish truth from falsity. Then, only you and I can distinguish what is mere happenstance from what is necessarily true, from what happens to be the case from that which must be.

If correct (it is, isn't it?) this raises a nice philosophical question. What is true about you? Is all truth about you happenstance—could it be other than it is? Or is there anything true about you that is necessary, essential and marks and measures the very meaning of what you are?

Again, only you and I can ask that; only you and I can know about that; only you and I are more than aware—we are conscious—only you and I can *know. Know what?* More than what happens to be the case, not simple information, but what must be the case.

5. Begin again. One of my favorite words: *salacious.* Words that sound *ush* at the end are, well, mouth-watering and delicious—like *delicious. Delicious* (Oh! Got to say it again!)

Satisfies my tongue, like a sip of water when mouth is dry. Tasty are words that end in *ish* like *cherish, flowerish, Irish. Uous* words make your tongue feel sexy: *sumptuous, mellifluous, ambiguous, contiguous, conspicuous, promiscuous.*

Silly fun: I*s there any dichotomous between hippopotamus and rhinoceros? Preposterous!* For the loveliest wordplay visit Ogden Nash: *The pelican ... can hold in his beak enough food for a week, but I'm damned if I know how the hell he can.*

Preposterous! Essayist Charles Krauthammer's favorite word exercises all your mouth muscles if you say it correctly. Shout the second syllable and your mouth becomes what preposterous means; Krauthammer liked that it bordered on being onomatopoetic.

My favorite? I think it is *maelstrom*. Why? Don't know. Such a serious word. But this is romantic stuff and self-indulgent (nice word!) *Preposterous* is a serious word, as is *serious*. I never remember how to pronounce *quixotic* until I remember it rhymes with *exotic* and *erotic*. All these words are very fetching. So is *fetching*.

The above is romantic and self-indulgent and sentimental about how words feel. Look inside yourself, set aside self-indulgence, turn off your romantic mood and find your classical mode, your need for objective truth, that which is undeniably true and necessary about the world ... and the truth about your place in it. Are you feeling self-indulgent or are you feeling the need to be a serious person?

6. A drum roll for words that want you to march for them: *Eudemonia, effervescence, eternity, ontological* (*onto-logical*; what is *logical* about *ontos*—ancient Greek for *being*—not just existence but essentialness). Much of philosophy marches to the beat of *ontology*, convinced that to know things we need more than brute factual information. We need to know not just *that* they are and *how* they are, but more, *what* and *why* they are.

The ancient Greeks—who brought our western civilization to be—want to know the *logic* of things. *Logic*, from *logos*, Greek for *word*. And the Greeks are very aware that this can only be done in and through language, and only by you and I who possess and are possessed by the power of language and its propositional truth. Reminds of Ernest Hemingway's *Prose is architecture, not decoration, and the baroque is over.*

7. Some words taste good and sound deliciously. Some words are hard on the mouth ... and on the heart. *Horror:* not only difficult to pronounce but offers no sweetness to enrich the soul. I think that *horror* is

a horrible word. I do not like *huddle* and *muddle;* they are of meaning too indistinct. *Riddle* and *fiddle* are okay.

Muddle is ambiguous, fuzzy of meaning (I like *ambiguous*). What marks a situation to be muddled? I do not know. The ambiguity of *fiddle* is clear and distinct. As a noun *fiddle* names a musical instrument. As a verb, *to fiddle around* is the titillating invitation to the devil's musical instrument.

Ambiguity vs. ambivalence, a nice distinction. And a moment's reflection to realize that this insight into reality can be done with and in, and only in, language. Language, the only serious and significant access to the nature of reality, despite our preference for the easy gathering of information, sensation by eye and ear to form impressions of how things appear.

I said *serious and significant.* To pierce the deceptive veil of brute ambiguous fact (*how red is that apple?*) we have ... what? What but science, poetry, and, yes, philosophy: all linguistic revelation of the reality that lies hidden behind appearance.

Yes, some words bring brute fact, *that's a stand of trees* (*the ambiguity: how many trees make a stand?*). But clear and distinct meaning only in reality revealing language: **These woods are lovely, dark and deep; but I have promises to keep; and miles to go before I sleep.**

The difference: the former (*a stand of trees*) classically reports appearance, a fact; the latter (*these woods are lovely, dark and deep; but I have promises to keep; and miles to go before I sleep*) romantically explores its human significance.

8. An entire class of words suffer a special sort of ambiguity because they are so intimately tied to our empirical sensible experience: the random, disconnected flow of impressions by sight and sound. Examine

the language in which we report empirical encounter with the appearance things make to eye and ear, etc. You say that you, too, see that the apple is red. How do we know if the red-I-see is the same, or even like, the red you see?

We do not. We cannot. Ambiguity wraps everything seen or heard or tasted or smelled in egocentric mystery.

Is the red we see determined by the apple and objectively true of it, or determined by how our eye happens to work? Whales and dolphin eyes lack the cones that allow us to see color and they see in black and white. Again, is the red we see determined by the apple and objectively true of it, or determined by how our eye happens to work?

9. Their dual function: romantically, words-as-music or classically, words in their primary logical purpose as purveyors of truth. Language that sings, the musical romance of words, and on the other hand, words, the vehicle that delivers truth to the understanding, rendering reality intelligible.

Words, in proper logical form, intend the truth of the world as nothing else does. That's right: no words, no proposition, no truth. That is, linguistic truth remains hidden behind helplessly received appearance. But there is so much more to truth than information that rocks are hard, snow is cold and grass is green.

10. A common romantic error is to say *My Truth* or *True to them* as though truth lies within us, subjective, of emotional weight, a psychological state. Philosophers call that the error of *Psychologism*, as though truth were a function of how someone feels about things. Psychologism is a logical error born of romantic excess.

The classical truth about words: Meanings, these and only these, are true or false; Meaning is a function of words working to declare about the world; Truth is a function of meaning.

No meaning, no truth. Example. Consider *twelve is unhappy*. True? False? Neither! *Twelve is unhappy* has no meaning to be true or false. *Twelve is the sum of five and seven*. Ah! First meaningful, and happily a meaning that is true.

11. Some words perform like punctuation, un-romantic, classical, like form-fits-function Bauhaus design, logical and punctilious. The conjunctions *and*, *but*, and *or*, the definite and indefinite articles *the*, *a* and *an* are drums in a marching band compelling us to step to the beat of the prose.

Classically punctilious words, like good punctuation, clarify and make distinct, enhance intelligibility, enable the truth. But then comes the terrible trouble with the word *The*.

The is often used to choose some one particular thing to talk about, *the highest mountain*. Or, *the* can refer indiscriminately to any among a group of things as, *the reader of this book* ... But one sort of truth begins when the definite article, *the*, selects an individual to talk about (the subject), and brings words to truth by predicating of that individual, that which creates a true or false assertion, as in *The Man Who Shot Liberty Valence*.

12. Trouble begins when *the* selects some individual particular thing that does not exist. Consider, says Bertrand Russell in *On Denoting: The present king of France*. Obviously, there is no such thing; therefore, anything you say about the present king of France, anything you predicate of this non-existent subject, is—must be—false. The trouble: the denial of any false statement must be—by the logical nature of truth—true; just as the denial of any true statement must be false. If it is true that the apple is red, then it must be false that the apple is not red—and vice versa.

The denial of a false statement, if accurate, must be true.

Everyone will agree that saying *the present king of France is bald* is false, However, the denial, *the present king of France is not bald* is just as false! How can that be! Oi vey!

Review. *The present king of France* is bald is an assertion of meaning clear enough to be easily recognized as false. *The present King of France is bald* is of proper subject/predicate form, predicates properly, meaningfully, asserting that the subject is a bald person. However, its denial is just as false!

13. Existential angst over one little word. *The* cannot select as subject a non-existent and then meaningfully speak truly (or falsely) about it!

That defies the very idea of truth! Truth always arises when a relevant predicate, some characteristic or quality, is ascribed to a subject. *So-and-so is such-and-such* is the form and is the structural skeleton of truth. That skeleton, the *form*, needs only the meat, the *matter*, of a mutually relevant subject and predicate, named or described, for propositional meaning and truth to arise.

14. That's right. Things are out-there in the world and the ideas and impressions of them are in us, but the truth is neither out-there nor in us. So where is truth? A nice insight into the benefit that philosophy teaches us how to deal with perplexity. Questions perplex, not because we don't have the answer, but because we do not understand the nature of the question well enough.

The question is not *where* is truth, but *what* is truth. Truth should not be objectified as a thing, like the things we think to be out-there and the ideas of them that are in us. Do not objectify truth; do not think of truth as an entity; truth is accurately thinking and speaking in subject/predicate language allowing our uniquely human relationship with the (our) world. Namely, of all creatures, only we can intend and reveal the essential reality of things.

Truth is not a thing; it cannot be located, truth is not *here* or *there*; it is the light of intelligibility; and no other creature, only you and I, can bring the light of truth to reveal the intelligibility of all that occupies our experience of the world.

What a responsibility!

15. Can we speak meaningfully about things that do not exist? I think so. It is true that sleuth extraordinaire Sherlock Holmes loves his Meerschaum pipe and values the help and support of his friend, Dr. Watson. That is true: correct? That they (Holmes, his pipe, Watson) do not exist mean that they are not real? Perhaps non-existents are real in their own realm; let's call it *subsistence*. So argued The Austrian philosopher, Alexus Meinong (My-nong), whose theory of non-existent reality urged Russell to his *On Denoting*.

Russell's *On Denoting* became the touchstone for the birth and development of twentieth century British philosophy, by Russell and his followers that urge from (Russell's and Meinong's time, first decade of the twentieth century) to now, the oh-so-British *Linguistic Analytic Philosophy*.

Linguistic Analytic Philosophy. It analyzes all philosophical questions as puzzles of language, to be solved or resolved or best understood as problems—not of the world or of our understanding of the world (we have science for that), but of the nature and structure of the language in which philosophical questions are posed!

Its historical roots: the British Enlightenment of the eighteenth century, led by John Locke, and, under the supreme influence of David Hume. Its primary principle: Existence is the hallmark of reality. Analytic philosophy dismisses the possibility of non-existent significance as nothing but metaphysical fog obscuring the correct empiricist view of things. The empiricist revolution of the English enlightenment two centuries ago by John Locke and David Hume gave us the truth of things. This view pervades the English-speaking world from then to now, and, dear reader, I suspect it is yours.

Not mine.

16. So influential is Russell's paper, reacting to Meinong's proposal for a non-existing but subsisting reality that from then on, this major division exists between two competing schools of philosophical thought: English-speaking (classical) empiricism (only what exists is meaningful) and French/German (romantic) rationalism.

Worthy of your consideration: comparing the contrast between these two oh-so-different ways to understand your relationship to the world; nothing else so succinctly and completely forms your philosophical view of things... and of yourself.

17. The first philosophical question: As to things that occupy our experience of the world, which access marks and measures their reality? Are things real as they appear to the eye and ear, revealing their reality to our physical senses? Or is reality hidden behind the deceptive veil of appearance and apprehended only by the understanding that which intends their essential nature?

That is, is the truth of them marked by and advertised in their existence? Or is the truth of things hidden behind physical and factual appearance, a matter measured by their essential nature?

My view: what is true of things is so much more than simple, brute, factual information: that rocks are hard, that snow is cold, that grass is green. What is true, dear reader, about you? That you are blond or brunette? Tall or short? Young or old? Or how well achieved is your femininity or masculinity?

Dear reader: I think I know your view; can you guess where I stand on this?

18. The second philosophical question: Are there different sorts of truth? One kind of truth speaks to the circumstance of a thing's existence ... its happenstance, though, could be other than it happens to be, like *the door is open* and *you are reading this essay*. Philosophers call these *synthetic* (the predicate adds information not contained in the subject) and therefore informative.

Necessary truth is so different a kind of truth they ought not be both called *truth*. Unlike truths of happenstance, necessary truth is innate in human understanding and does not depend upon eye and ear to be gathered into our awareness: *a straight line is the shortest distance between two points*; *of three things if one is bigger than the second, and the second is bigger than the third, then the first is, must be, necessarily, bigger than the third*.

I know, that was difficult to follow, so why bother? Aha! The ultimate truth-question for philosophy, *as to being a person, are there any necessary truths?* Or, as we tend to think, is everything about us but happenstance and accidental?

The purpose of philosophy is to investigate whether there be truths about the human condition that are not mere happenstance but both necessary and informative.

19. Truth-contingent vs. truth-necessary is the most significant and the most overlooked distinction about truth.

Happenstance, rudely and importantly, overwhelms helplessly receptive senses. Apprehension of necessity requires discrimination and choice.

Truth-necessary requires the discrimination and choice of the educated understanding that renders intelligible the random flow of sensible, but unintelligible impression.

What *happens* to be the case vs. what *must be* the case are such different truths, they ought not both be called *truth*.

Why does the ordinary pre-philosophical view value happenstance over necessity? What *happens* to be the case is, of course, informative but could be other than it happens to be. Happenstance, factual information, is, of course, so easy to gather into our sensibility as it (I think so rudely) intrudes upon our helpless organs of sense.

The grandest philosophical goal: to understand how it is that we are the only creatures capable of apprehending knowledge that is both necessary and informative! For more, see the essay *Knowability*.

Does God Exist?

1. The most romantic and delectable and ingenious argument for the existence of God, the *Ontological Argument,* convinces but makes an awful mistake. Let me tread carefully, this is a minority view.

The method is modern. Ever since the Frenchman Rene Descartes and Irishman George Berkeley, to think modern is to begin an inquiry into *x* with, *What does x mean?* Begin here: *What does God mean?* God *means*: *the most perfect being that can be conceived.*

The Ontological Argument: *If He did not exist then He would not, could not, be perfect. He is perfect. Therefore, He must exist.* Does this convince? Well, *yes,* and, *no.*

We are so sure we know what we mean by *existence*—means the same as *real,* right? But, dear reader, I ask that we consider *existence* to be a troubling notion when applied to a perfect God.

Concentrate on what God *means.* By definition, perfection is the mark and measure of His very being. I find the Ontological Argument irresistible as based on *meaning.* God *means*: that perfect entity which is omniscient, all-knowing, and omnipotent, all powerful. That is, there is no limit to God's power and no limit to His knowledge.

Focus on what God *means,* and discover that divinity not only *is,* but *must be,* real. Otherwise, the world we live in and all the things it contains cannot be explained. The argument proves that divinity is real, needed to explain how and why things exist, but that does not mean that God *exists*.

I know, I know. You, dear reader, think existence and reality mean the same.

I am in the minority in my view that existence and reality are not the same, that reality extends farther than existence and includes much that does not exist. *Does God exist?* If He does, does He suffer the tribulations shared by all existing things?

I think the Ontological Argument proves that divinity is real—must be real—as the most powerful explanation of why things exist.

2. *Being*: not an easy notion for our ordinary way of thinking about the world, about existence and reality. The most useful philosophical notion of *being* comes from twentieth-century German philosopher Martin Heidegger: *that which makes an entity understandable.* What a lovely notion! Reality is not a matter of existence but of intelligibility.

Being, in Greek, *ontos*; hence the *Ontological Argument.* Understand what God means and know He must be real. The full understanding of divinity proves that it is real, not that it exists. Reality and existence *are not* the same.

The being of divinity cannot be denied. Divinity is the only persuasive explanation by which to understand that the existing world *is*, as inspired to be by each thing's full and complete explanation, which explanation, when full and complete, is divine.

3. The misconception, or so argues my minority view, is our pervasive, but mistaken, devotion to existence as the ultimate measure of the real. Indeed, we think (I bet, dear reader, you too) reality and existence are

the same! But much reality, I argue, does not exist. Non-existing real things: triangles, Sherlock Holmes, unicorns.

How do I know there are non-existing realities? *I know truths about them.* Is that not the test of reality? It is true that triangles have three sides. Are they not real? Their reality is to be contrasted with squares and circles. Sherlock Holmes is an exemplary detective. Would he be a better detective if he existed? It is true that unicorns have one mid-forehead horn, whether they exist or not ... correct?

4. The so compelling Ontological Argument bases itself on the ancient Greek *ontos*, for *being*. *Being* in Martin Heidegger's sense: the condition for and structure of reality, the essence of being-ness itself, whether existing or not.

Compelling? Here's why, the Ontological Argument, based on the meaning of being: *What does God mean? The Lord, by definition is the greatest that can be conceived. If He does not exist, then He could be greater still.* Suppose He does not exist? Then He would be greater if he did exist – goes the argument. Therefore, based on what God *means*, he not only *is*, but He *must* be. I do not agree that *means* He *exists*.

To this I say: *Yes, divinity must be*, but I do not know that it exists. Indeed, I am sure it does not. Things that exist flood the senses with their appearance. Is divinity red or green like a MacIntosh apple?

5. Ever since the English Enlightenment and the rise of the so influential ...

(How influential? All of us—I suspect that you, too, dear reader—are thoroughly empiricist in your understanding of our world.)

... English-speaking empiricism—existence is regarded as definitive for rendering things real—so regarded by everyone I know. So regarded, I think, by you. Not me.

6. We think *it exists*, ah! That is its primary and most significant characteristic! After all, the appearance emanating from its existence makes it present to eye and ear, and, we think, to *be*, to be *real*. We think existence is the metric of reality. We are all children of the so influential empiricist English Enlightenment, and all in the English-speaking world are unreasonably devoted to this empiricist prejudice: existence and reality are the same.

My minority argument is that existence does *not* add anything to our understanding of what makes a thing to be what it is. I argue that what makes a thing to be what it is, *is* its meaning. How real? How well does it accomplish and achieve what it means to be one of its kind. And existence? That's a blemish. On what? On reality!

Existence is a blemish on reality? Here's why. Existing things get bumped, bruised, age, rot and die. If it exists, then it is constantly changing, searching for a better way to deal with the hardships of surviving the challenges of the harsh and demanding physical world.

Ah! Better read that again! Isn't it correct? If it did not exist, then it would not get bumped, bruised, age, rot and die. Let's look again at the conclusion of the Ontological Argument: *God exists*. Existing things get bumped, bruised, age, rot and die. Their eternal *Form*, the full and complete definition, their divine source, does not exist and does not suffer the hardships of existence; nor does the omnipotent and omniscient mind of God.

7. Off-putting about the Ontological Argument: It wants to prove that the Lord *exists*. For anything to exist, including the Lord, it must, by definition, for this is what existence *means*, be located in space and

time, be of a color, a physical shape, a taste, a smell, etc. And I think it is blasphemy to think this about the Lord.

Ah, but is He real? An entirely different question. Notice, it does not matter to me whether you call Him God, or, for secularists, *divinity*. To phrase the question in a way I can answer: *Is Divinity real?* Absolutely! I learned from Plato that the Divine, the Good, the *best possibility* not only *is*, but *must* be, in order to explain the origin of and the source for this existing world.

Why? The Divine, the Good, the *good-est* one, the best-possible, is rendered intelligible by a thing's full and complete definition. Plato called it the *Form,* the full and most beautiful expression of what a thing *means* which blueprints, inspires and makes possible things to be(come).

That is, both Plato and Aristotle are undeniably correct that how-*good*-a-one-it-is defines the reality of each individual, particular thing.

8. The Ontological Argument convinces: The Divine *must* be real, and it explains why things exist. The Good, the Excellent, the Beautiful are the originating source that inspires things to be. Their blueprinting creative power answers the question: *Why are there things? Where do they come from?*

The Ontological Argument convinces when it argues from *meaning.* The Lord of Holy Scripture *means* that entity, *perfect,* all knowing, with no limit to His power. Divine omniscience thinks the full and complete definition of things. That thinking has the force of omnipotent unlimited power. Then things cannot help but burst into existence.

How becoming! How lovely! How romantic! Existence is an act of love! Things exist because they are inspired to be by the full and compelling expression of their essential meaning.

9. My view is that divinity *is* real. But, I see no reason to believe that He *exists*. However, all existence comes to be from His omniscience and omnipotence. The divine expression of what things mean explains the origination of things.

And that is how I understand:

> **I do not believe in God, and I am not an atheist.**

Albert Camus, *Notebooks, 1951 – 1959.*

Played All the Cards in His Hand

> ... [P]eople get married young. They go to work early and in ten years exhaust the experience of a lifetime. A thirty-year-old workman has already "played all the cards in his hand." He awaits the end between his wife and children. His joy has been sudden and merciless, as has been his life ... [which] is not to be built up, but to be burned up. Stopping to think and become better is out of the question.
>
> <div align="right">Albert Camus. "Summer in Algiers" <i>Myth of Sisyphus and Other Essays.</i></div>

1. If it is true that we all live in the conventions and the pretensions of our private lives with family and friends and in the conventions and pretensions of our public lives of work and recreation, then God help us if they have run their course. *Played all the cards in his hand;* his life has run its course.

> *Everyone has three lives: a public life, a private life and a secret life.*
>
> Gabriel García Marquez.

> *I want to be with those who know secret things or else alone.*
>
> Rainer Maria Rilke.

Satanic, inexplicable, tempestuous, wanton with wild random desire and uncontrollable impulse that effervesces like a volcano bursting through the earth's mantle is our carefully guarded secret life. We are frightened and amazed. Thank goodness we have our public and private lives to show everyone. But the devil entices us to indulge our secret life.

2. *L'Étranger*, an important part of the Camus opus that won the Nobel Prize for Literature in 1957, is translated in America as *The Stranger*, but more correctly in England as *The Outsider*.

Outside... what?

How strange is Meursault, main character of *L'Étranger*. He is outside all expectation and convention. Strange Meursault surprises himself as much as he surprises us. Like the babe in his crib, he is barely aware of himself, unaware of what might happen to him, and of what he might do next. He does not think, and is surprised by what happens. In a sense, he is less than conscious.

Stopping to think and become better is out of the question. We innocents are unable to think, to deliberate, to choose the evil that Satan plans for us. This view denies the tale of divinely innocent Eve. Beware the apple and be tempted by the devilish snake *to know*.

Meursault is as innocent as Eve, but falls to evil because of it. The biblical Eve and Meursault: two opposing notions of how and why there is evil. Scripture is correct: Knowledge has something, *everything*, to do with evil.

Meursault does everything casually, nothing deliberately. Deliberation is *out of the question*. He murders, but casually. It is as though he did not do it—as though it *happened* to him. Did the devil do it? I mean: the devilish evil of innocence.

Meursault is not conscious. By that I mean he does not, *cannot*, consider and evaluate consequences. Unconscious, like an innocent babe, the subconscious rises up and his secret life takes over, surprising everyone, including himself.

Every circumstance he finds himself in just *is*—with no moral weight or significance. No consciousness of right and wrong, so no conscience. Like the beast and the innocent babe, he has no self, no self-awareness, nothing to regret. Nice insight: no beast, none but man can regret.

3. Meursault has no public and no private life. He lives his secret life in public, out in the open; We are both titillated and revolted. We feel sorry for him, and for ourselves. We want to forgive him, and ourselves ... *the devil made him do it.* We worry: Will the devil work on us next?

4. Camus asks that we be open-minded enough—but he knows we are not honest enough—to face the truth that the search for *meaning-in-life* is hopeless and foolish. Nevertheless, we pursue the *meaningful life* because, well, how else to go on?

Is not innocence, with no capacity to consider consequence, the condition of possibility for evil? Meursault is disconnected from the world which busies our very busy private and public lives. Crazed with unending self-indulgence, Meursault's insanity is like a child falling to evil within devilish innocence.

Perhaps we need to pay more attention to the Christian notion that evil is not an existent, but an absence. God sees to it that things *are*. That is, He sees to it that they are *good* as measured by how good-a-one they are, how well achieved an example they are of their kind. Meursault's evil is not a presence, but an absence. Absent in Meursault is this sense of *good*.

That is the ecclesiastical puzzle as to why God would permit evil. Theologians answer, *He does not! Everything he creates is inspired by, molded and formed by His full and divine understanding of the Good.* But in the full good garden of His creation, why did the Lord make Eve innocent? Because, by the Grace of God, His gift of free will takes precedence in distinguishing man from the beast—even though that opens the door to man's evil mischief and misdemeanors.

Meursault has no will, free or otherwise. He is Eve before the Fall. I think mankind had to be put out of the Garden so that now, with free will, he has consciousness, and a conscience. Anti-scriptural, but perhaps innocence is the condition of possibility that thwarts God's purpose. So much for our adoration of the innocent babe.

5. Meursault has no self-control, in good part because he has no control over his world. Like the child, he made no contribution to how his world is, so he has no responsibility for it or what he does in it or to it.

To apprehend and appreciate the good, to intend and deploy what is righteous requires consciousness; Meursault lacks the consciousness that makes us human, and, therefore, has no self-awareness, no self-consciousness, no self.

His world is a *fait accompli*, factual, fully formed before he arrives to it and finds it foisted upon him; He had nothing to do with its making, nothing to do with how he arrived to it, and therefore is not responsible for what he does in it or to it.

I am not the first to say this. See Simone de Beauvoir's *The Ethics of Ambiguity.*

Incapable of pretense, he is incapable of constructing a public or private life. Savor the famous opening line of *The Outsider: My mother died today, or maybe it was yesterday.*

6. Aware, but not conscious, Meursault cannot think. About what? About how to become better. Like the child and like the Nazi bureaucrat following orders, he can only do what Mommy, or some other exterior authority or inner impulse, makes him do. He can only play the cards he is dealt. Picking new cards is out of the question.

He lives behind bars, a prisoner in a jail cell of innocence. He cannot change his world, so he cannot change himself. His evil is primal; His life is a deal with the devil. Every joy is a surprise, unplanned, unexpected and merciless. Rare are those meaningful life-moments of discovery and appreciation for the beautiful, the excellent, and the sublime. That takes what the ancient Greeks called *arete*, virtue; but we are not born with a thirst for the excellent ... Meursault never developed it.

7. Like a babe in the crib, he has no plan, no goal. Simone de Beauvoir says, in *The Ethics of Ambiguity, The trouble with men is they begin as children* arriving to a world already fully constituted, helpless, with no cards to play, and hardly able to obey or disobey, but incapable of doing anything else.

Grow up and begin to think about becoming better, or more likely and more sadly, blindly obey the conventional demands of public and private life.

The uncomfortable truth: We would rather be comfortable and live in our pretentions than ask if our pretensions are worth living. What pretensions? Camus is not a sociologist, nor does he want to be called a philosopher. He thinks of himself as a storyteller, a raconteur, exposing the terrible, barebones truth.

8. To be successful is to successfully pretend and posture that we know about the good life. We are in charge of our private and public life. But our only honest life is our secret life, which rules us. Not easy: choosing to become what we want to be.

9. Meursault has no self-reflection, no self to try to make better. He has no public or private ego.

This is Freud's psychoanalytic distinction between ego, the self-aware self and our secret life, that Freud called the *id*. The id, *a cauldron of seething excitation,* is what we have called the secret life. Camus warns us to beware. If you do not pay attention, build it, make it better, life will burn up in the ashes of ennui.

Freud's *id*, the secret life, threatens when we have played all the cards in our public and private lives. Reminds of Shakespeare's warning that the world is a stage, and we are script-directed players filling out assigned roles.

10. Choose (!) how and what to be. Choose the cards, the roles you will play in your public and private life. *Choose*, says Camus, *to be*, to become the person you decide to be. You are the only creature capable of, and responsible for, doing this. Fail to choose and resigning to play the cards you are dealt, as do all non-human creatures, and risk losing the game of life before it is over.

Humanity is an exclusive club and should not be modeled after the life of the beast and explained in terms of behavior in response to environmental pressures enforced by habit. That sort of explanation is for non-human creatures. That explanation sees why the plant grows to the light, but cannot explain Meursault.

Meursault's debilitation, and yes, it is correct to say his insanity: He is incapable of making a choice about what to do, how to think. He does not know what to think, what to do to become a better person. Meursault is *aware* but not *conscious*.

11. Richard Mitchell would say that Meursault is, in a certain sense, *unconscious*. All sentience is *aware*, all living things are factually describable as ensconced in an interactive web of stimulus and response. Hail (or

damn) the social sciences that model our understanding of ourselves on the habitual behavior of the beast or the innocent baby.

Even the stream is *aware* by responding to the incline of the streambed down which it runs, appropriately, faster and slower ... correct? Like the stream, Meursault is aware of the factual circumstances in which he is entangled, but he cannot untangle, and suffers no sense of what is appropriate.

He does not qualify to be a sentient creature capable of surviving practical predicament. He is barely sentient, not even a beast behaving appropriately within the demands of physical circumstance.

We can be conscious, not just aware, but self-reflectively in charge of *getting better.* We are not just aware of what we are but conscious of what we might become.

The End

We are in postmodern times and past philosophy. Also gone: history, art, poetry, serious music. We do not know what to ask, what to honor. We do not know where we have been, so we do not know where to go.

We favor fact over value, information over insight. We know the world only by description of happenstance ... the combination of *happen* and *circumstance*.

Postmodern man does not analyze experience. The world is a happening place and now we *participate*. Everything is possible, and nothing is certain. We have lost the thirst to know. We are uniformed and doubt that we are formed by a soul.

In *The Medium is the Message,* Marshall McLuhan gives the flavor of the postmodern. *People don't actually read newspapers, they get into them every morning like a hot bath ...* We choose *movies rather than books; avant-garde movies rather than plotted realist movies that develop narrative and character; TV rather than radio; the modern feely-feely lifestyle rather than Victorian class structure.*

If it feels good, do it ... *rather than principled decision; sympathy and empathy rather than* tough love; *the romantic rather than the classic; ecstasy rather than science; music rather than mathematics.*

PHILOSOPHY IS NOT DIFFICULT ... WE ARE! | 241

A couple of centuries ago, two grand competing philosophical rhapsodies, empiricism vs. rationalism, energize the classical philosophical spirit. Then, in the late 1700s, Immanuel Kant's grand philosophic insight: *How we know determines what we know.* The flavor of contemporary thought romantic.

This subjectivism, Descartes to Kant, metastasizes by the late 1900s into a skepticism over the possibility of attaining objective truth. Now a thorough going relativism in all things that dooms the classical intellectual fervor.

The West sang an intellectual rhapsody, then the music died.

> *Helter Skelter in a* [postmodern] ***swelter***
>
> *We all got up to dance*
>
> *I saw Satan laughing with delight*
>
> *The day the music died*
>
> *I went down to the sacred store*
>
> *Where I'd heard the music years before*
>
> *But the man there said the music wouldn't play*
>
> *But not a word was spoken;*
>
> *The church bells all were broken*
>
> *And the three men I admire most:*
>
> *The father, son, and the holy ghost*
>
> *They caught the last train for the coast*

The day the music died.

    Mclean, Don, composer. *American Pie*. Musixmatch. 1971.

All this is said in the pre-postmodern voice, dedicated to the search for objective truth. A sad question, is anyone interested in the question: *Is a physical description of our situation enough to make us understand who and what we are?*

The end. The end of this book. The end of the western tradition. Stanford emeritus historian, Victor David Hanson, will have nothing more to write about after his just published (2024) scholarly study, *The End of Everything*.

The end of respect and appreciation for tradition, for the continuation over generations of cultural identity. The end of the search for the excellent and the sublime, not only to know who and what we are, but what we might become.

Postmodern man has no plan, no purpose. We have become like the audience of Japanese monster movies. The postmodern world looks like a fantasy film of inexplicable, disconnected bits. Postmodern concerns amount to little more than a silly, sick joke.

Acknowledgement

Pat and Terry made this book possible.

Wordsmith editor, Patrica Reginia, and manuscript manager Theresa Morgan made it possible to bring this to print.

Printed in the USA
CPSIA information can be obtained
at www.ICGtesting.com
LVHW010307100824
787870LV00009B/232